HIS VOICE IN TODAY'S WILDERNESS

GOD'S WAKE-UP CALL TO THE CHURCH

Barrie Creak

His Voice In Today's Wilderness
God's Wake-Up Call To The Church
by Barrie Creak

Printed in the United States of America

ISBN 9781600348792

Unless otherwise indicated, Bible quotations are taken from
The King James Version.

www.xulonpress.com

CONTENTS

INTRODUCTION

How do I begin to put into words what has been revealed to me through dreams and studying God's word so that you will want to read this book from cover to cover?

In this book you will find God's will for your life and come to understand the very purpose of life. You will find out which Christians will enter the kingdom of heaven and which won't and what it really means to be born again. You will learn the difference between having presumption and real faith for God's promises and how to reconcile faith and works. You will come to recognize God's true church and the deceived counterfeit church, and much more.

There are so many teachings that are charismatically delivered and books which present the author's thoughts yet lack the substance, authority and particularly the intent of the word of God. The content of this book which was inspired by dreams does not consist of my thoughts or ideas, but is built on more than 750 scriptures and based on the teachings of Jesus who taught not as the scribes, but as one having authority (Mt 7:29). The scripture references for each passage have been conveniently inserted into the text to enable them to be easily reviewed.

I have listened to so many Christians reading passages from the scriptures with no intonation in their voices, where the listeners certainly do not easily get a clear understanding of what has been written. Paul, speaking about *unknown tongues* establishes the importance of clarity citing the use of the trumpet in giving commands (1Cor 14:6-9). The readers themselves may not get the full import of what they have read: to them, the scriptures may appear to lack **LIFE** and **revelation,** and they may have a limited depth of understanding. I have therefore taken the liberty of placing emphasis on certain words in this book to help bring clarity to a passage. I humbly recommend that if you recognize yourself as being like the Ethiopian eunuch who was unable to understand a certain scripture (Act 8:26-31), then pray and ask the Holy Spirit to bring the passages of scripture in this book to life before you begin to read.

This book is not intended for light or casual reading like a novel, but for those whose hope is in the kingdom of God to study and meditate on the scriptural principles that it establishes so that they may understand and put into practice God's will for their lives.

The scribes and Pharisees of Jesus' day thought they were righteous because they kept the Mosaic Law and that God was their Father because they were descendants of Abraham. They were wrong on both points as Jesus revealed to them. He called them hypocrites and said that their righteousness was only an outward appearance (Mt 23:28) and told others that they would not enter the kingdom of heaven unless their righteousness exceeded that of the scribes and Pharisees (Mt 5:20). He told other believing Jews that even though they were the biological descendants of Abraham, they were not his children because they did not do the works of Abraham, and that in fact they were children of the devil (Jn 8:31-44); – a revelation that would shake the faith of many Christians today, even though Paul warned the gentile believers about this very issue. (Ro 11:17-23)

There are multitudes in the church today, both leaders and followers, who believe they have been made righteous solely by the atoning work of Christ on the cross, and others who believe they have eternal life because of their relationship with God through Jesus Christ his Son, yet so many of them have not correctly understood the scriptures and fall into the same category as those scribes and Pharisees. John makes it very clear that it is only those who **do** acts of righteousness who are righteous, and that those who do not are children of the devil (1Jn 3:7-10). Jesus said that those who are truly related to him are those who **do** the will of his Father, (Lu 8:19-21) and that only these will enter the kingdom of heaven. (Mt 7:21)

When some scribes and Pharisees who considered themselves to be righteous murmured because Jesus was eating with tax collectors and sinners, he told them that it is not those who are healthy that need a doctor, but those who are sick. He had not come to call the righteous but the sinners to repentance (Lu 5:30-32). The purpose of this book is to give light to those in darkness, to replace error with truth and understanding through God's word. To give readers the opportunity to judge themselves against the unchangeable rock of God's word.

This book will challenge many erroneous concepts by exposing them to the light of God's word. It will help readers to see themselves as God sees them, not as they see themselves or even as others see them, for that is frequently a deception. When we review the words that Jesus dictated to John for the seven churches of Asia nearly two thousand years ago, we read that the **church** of Laodicea saw itself as rich and in need of nothing, whereas God saw it as wretched, miserable, poor, blind and naked (Rev 3:17). The **church** of Sardis was seen by others as a church that was alive, but God saw it as being dead (Rev 3:1). Both churches were called to repent or suffer the consequences. Why should we think that churches and Christians today are somehow immune to deceptions and error? This is the devil's work and he is good at it. Jesus said that if it was possible even the very elect would be deceived. (Mt 24:24)

The purpose of God's correction is always to give the opportunity for repentance just as Jesus did with the church of Laodicea (Rev 3:19), but sadly scripture indicates that many will not change, and will one day hear Jesus say to them 'I never knew you: depart from me, you workers of iniquity.' (Mt 7:23)

I encourage you to use this book as a mirror. Look at your reflection honestly and see yourself as God does, judging yourself honestly with the word of God to see if you really are fit for the kingdom of heaven. Let your mind be like a clean page with no writing on it; turn back the clock 2000 years and hear Jesus speaking to you afresh, for minds cluttered with presumptuous promises make it difficult to receive corrective truth., This is why Jesus and Paul in particular had such difficulty in getting many people of their day to receive the truth; their minds were already filled with religious traditions and error.

For the sake of the church, it is my deepest desire to help reassert the truth of God's word which in so many instances has been replaced with traditions and theology that run contrary to the teachings of Jesus.

'Lord, this is your work not mine, you have shown me these truths to awaken your church so that many will not miss the mark and perish. I ask you to help them to put aside their own understanding and any misconceptions, and open their spiritual eyes and ears to receive your words and understand them with their heart as you intended, that they might be converted and healed.' (Mt 13:15)

DREAMS

G od says that in the last days he will pour out his Spirit upon mankind. Sons and daughters will prophesy, young men shall see visions and old men will dream dreams. (Act 2:17)

By the grace of God, I was brought to a knowledge of my need for salvation in 1979. I quickly discovered that I had an insatiable appetite for the word of God. I wanted to learn and understand as much as I could about this salvation that I had neglected and rejected for the first thirty one years of my life. Everything changed dramatically overnight. Gross sins such as Paul lists as 'the works of the flesh' fell away immediately. I committed my life to God and to the work of the kingdom in my home town, where I became a leader in a small Fellowship, and soon found myself teaching others what I had learned from the word of God.

As the years passed by I became disenchanted because of criticism, division and strife in the body of Christ, and so I buried myself in my secular job. Not even my wife and children saw much of me, let alone my bible, which was often left unopened from one Sunday to the next.

It took God to awaken me from this condition of hopelessness. In July 2001 I had a dream. Before I share the dream with you, let me explain that for many years I had been a very deep sleeper, never waking up in the night, even when the babies were crying to be fed. My wife used to wonder how I could just fall asleep in the evenings with the noise and turmoil of all the children in the house. Throughout this period in my life I never remembered dreaming, even though we are told that we all dream.

At the time I had this dream I was to all intents and purposes backslidden. I still attended church faithfully, I had not reverted to gross sin, but I had stopped actively seeking the Lord and his kingdom, and had not been praying or studying his word. So when I awoke one morning with this dream fresh in my mind, I knew it was something out of the ordinary. It was God's wake up call for me.

My wake up Dream

In my dream I appeared to be in the communal changing room of a sports hall with many other people. We were all putting on robes; theirs were all white but mine was brown. A bell sounded which was the signal to leave the room. We all filed out into a wide but angular corridor that had many doors leading off it on the opposite side. All the people went through one or other of these various different doors, but I stood in the corridor wondering which door I was supposed to go through. The people filed quickly through the doors and all the doors were shut. I alone was left standing in the corridor.

The dream is self-explanatory; it is a variation of the parable of *The Ten Virgins*. (Mt 25:1-13)

My dream was showing me that if I remained in my present condition, when the time comes to meet the bridegroom I would not be ready. Those who were ready, shown by the purity of their white robes (Rev 19:7-8), went in and the door was shut. I was left outside like one of the foolish virgins.

You can imagine how such a dream startled me and brought me to a place of immediate repentance. My whole life began to change again from that day, but it didn't mean that my robe had instantly changed from brown to white. It takes time for the heart to fully change even if the mind tells you that it should. It is only as you apply yourself to that change that your need for further change is revealed to you.

Now many people say they have heard from God. They have had a dream or a vision and God told them this or God told them that. God does not expect us to accept everything that people tell us; we are to be discerning. If such dreams and visions originate with God then their content is prophetic, and Paul writes that we are to judge prophecy (1Cor 14:29). As a guide we should compare it with the written word of God and with what other established prophets have said. Consider the accuracy of any previous prophecies from this same person, for there are many who make short term prophecies which time reveals to be false. We are not called to blindly accept whatever brothers or sisters tell us that they have heard from God, no matter how sincere or prominent they may be, for their words might have originated from their own mind rather than from God. To quote an old saying: the proof of the pudding is in the eating.

John warns us to *try the spirits* (1Jn 4:1). This test he gives is not whether the *person* confesses that Jesus Christ has come in the flesh but whether or not the *spirit* confesses that Jesus Christ has come in the flesh. It is a test of their spirit not their lips. We can get anybody to *say* that Jesus Christ has come in the flesh. This is not the test, for even the demon possessed can say this (Lu 4:34, Act 19:15). How does a person's spirit confess that Jesus Christ is come in the flesh? Not just by what they say, but by the change in their lives. Is the life of Jesus Christ truly manifest in *their* flesh? Has *their* spirit come into agreement with the Spirit of God? Do *their* works truly verify that this person is walking in a new way of life, in God's ways? Examine their personal fruit.

Sometimes the origin of a prophecy is not obvious unless it is revealed to someone with a gifting in that area; in which case it should neither be rejected nor accepted, but held lightly and watched to see whether it is fulfilled. If it is personal, as was my dream, we should make sure that we as individuals get right with God in accordance with scripture otherwise, as in my dream the door will be shut and it will be too late.

Over the following three years I had a further six dreams concerning the kingdom of God. It is one that I had in January 2004 about a wedding which is the focus of this book.

My wedding dream

Just before awakening on this morning I dreamt that I was in a large reception area that might have been like that in the foyer of a grand hotel or a large hall. There were several brides all dressed in their wedding gowns. The brides were of all shapes and sizes and wore wedding gowns that seemed to be the fashion of the day, some with bare midriffs, others with shapes cut out of them. My first reaction was that there was about to be a mass wedding ceremony with all these brides being married simultaneously.

I observed two men walking amongst these brides, one of whom I understood to be a bridegroom, the other I suspected was his best man. They appeared to be looking for his bride, but it was apparent that they could not find her amongst all the brides that were there. I heard these brides talking amongst themselves, and saying that this bridegroom was incorrectly dressed. I then saw that his trouser belt was removed, and I saw a pair of scissors re-shaping it.

At this point in my dream the whole scene went blank, just as though I had been watching a film and the power had been switched off, then moments later the vision returned. This time there was only one bride, she was dressed in a traditional white bridal gown and was standing with the bridegroom that I had previously seen. She was clearly his bride, the one he had been looking for.

My observations were as follows.

I was being shown a picture of the church. Those who would be the bride of Christ were many, but they were not *one*. Jesus will return for one bride. They had not made themselves ready, because they were not clothed according to the bridegroom's instructions and expectations as his bride will be. Instead, they were dressed in what seemed good to them and the fashion of the day.

The bridegroom was none other than Jesus, and the other man I assumed to be the Holy Spirit. These would-be-brides had the audacity to presume that rather than conforming themselves to the image of God's Son, they would conform him to **their** image. They wanted to change the bridegroom's belt, the belt of truth representing the truth of God's word, and refashion it to suit **their** dictates. They did not accept that the truth of God's word does not change.

Although these brides had presented themselves for the wedding, I realized that these were not Jesus' bride, although they thought they should have been, for Jesus will not return for many brides, but one bride that has made herself ready. They could be likened to the *foolish virgins*, they were not acceptable. When I eventually saw the bridegroom with his bride, I realized that this bride was *one*, and had made herself ready, she was properly clothed. (Rev 19:7-8)

Let me emphasize that it is the bride who makes herself ready, just as Esther prepared herself for King Ahasuerus. The scripture here does not focus on the finished work of Christ on the cross, but on the work of the bride in **preparing herself**.

For several years I did not understand the significance of the interlude in this dream, but later came to realize that I was first being shown the current condition of the church, much of which is not ready for the Lord, and then shortly afterwards, the bride that had made herself ready for the marriage when the Lord returns. I did not know what became of the former brides. I now understand that the interlude is a short window of opportunity that God has graciously given for the church to put away its own doctrines and traditions and prepare itself in accordance with the bridegroom's instructions.

Just as some of the priests in Jesus' day became obedient to the faith, so some of these former brides will change and become part of the true latter bride, but not all. How many repent depends on them, and how long they have only God knows. This one thing we should note, that immediately before we are told that the bride has made herself ready (Rev 19:7), we read that God is still calling his people out of Babylon (Rev 18:4).

Paul emphasizes the need for this separation for those who would be the sons and daughters of God (2Cor 6:14-18), and the need for purity if we are to avoid the anger of God (Eph 5:1-8). Many scriptures tell us that before his return much of the church will be spiritually asleep, and like the former brides in my dream they will not be ready. (Mk 13:35-36; Rom 13:11-12; Eph 5:14-16; 1The 5:6)

It is only recently that I have come to realize that this dream was given to me for one purpose, as a wake-up call to the church. To declare the truth of God's word so that it will act as a warning to those who have believed in part and yet been blinded by the adversary into thinking they are ready when they are not.

In the light of this dream I set myself the task of reviewing the scriptures. It did not take me very long to realize that the scriptures on which many in the church base their hope of salvation come mainly from **our** interpretation of the writings of the apostle Paul, but when I started to review the teachings of Jesus I realized that the hope of salvation that many have is without adequate foundation and therefore presumptuous, and is giving countless thousands a false hope of eternal life.

This book is dedicated to showing the reader their true spiritual condition as seen through the eyes of the one who will be our judge, so that those who need to change, as I did, can do so whilst there is still time. It has taken me seven years to come to the place where I realized that although **my** wake up dream was personal, this one was for the church and I had to write all this down for others to read. I do not know how short the time is, so if you recognize that you have a need to change then don't delay, take swift action (Heb 4:11), for time is of the essence.

If these words of Jesus leave you realizing that you still have some way to go, don't despair or faint at the task ahead, take one step at a time and understand that because God loves you he has given you these words at this time to enable you to make any necessary heart changes. Like the *Prodigal Son* (Lu 15:20), as you take steps towards God by cleansing your hands and purifying your hearts, he will run to meet you. (Jas 4:8)

WHO'S CALLING
THE SHOTS?

Who created the earth? God did. It's his earth to do with as he pleases. God didn't just create the earth because he was bored and wanted something to do, he had a purpose; he wanted to replicate heaven on earth just for mankind that he had created.

We read that in the beginning God created all things, culminating in the creation of man to whom he gave dominion over his earth. Man was given the job of a caretaker over God's creation, and was given instructions - be fruitful and fill the earth and subdue it. (Gen 1:28) However, he was not completely at liberty to do just as he pleased; he was told that if he ate of the fruit of the tree of the knowledge of good and evil then dying he would die. (Gen 2:17) Death was not instant but it had been triggered. Why wasn't it instant? As always, it was to give man time to repent.

The story is familiar, Adam and Eve disobeyed God and were expelled from their garden paradise. Now we need to understand that although God had given man dominion, it was only as a caretaker under his ever watchful eye. Man was and always will be under God's authority and is called to do as God directs him or face the consequences. In this case, Adam and Eve lost their position – they got the sack, rather like the parable Jesus told of the *Unjust Steward*. (Lu 16:1)

God always is and always will be in overall control and is ever watchful to bring his purposes to pass. As time progressed man grew further and further away from God until in his heart he only ever harboured evil thoughts that came to him. (Gen 6:5)

It was not God's purpose to have his earth corrupted with evil, so with the exception of the **one** righteous man, Noah, his family and the creatures in the Ark, he destroyed all land based life. God started again with Noah, and gave him the same instruction as Adam – be fruitful and multiply and replenish the earth, (Gen 9:1) but as time went by, the descendants of Noah found a region they liked in the land of Shinar and decided they wouldn't continue on to replenish the earth, they determined to disobey God's instruction and stay. They built a waterproof tower just in case God went back on his word never to flood the whole earth again because of their rebellion (Gen 11:1-4). Again the story is familiar, God confounded their language which resulted in them being scattered over the face of the earth so that they would fulfil his instructions and his purposes.

God started again with Abraham to whom he also gave instructions. Abraham obeyed and followed God's instructions, resulting in God promising to bless him and multiply his seed (Gen 12:1-4). He promised to give Abraham the land to which he led him, which is far more extensive than the Israel of today (Gen 13:14-15). After the split between Abraham and his nephew Lot, Lot went to live in Sodom and Gomorrah, but the men there were wicked. It was not in God's purposes to leave this wickedness in his earth, so when their sin had become too great to ignore, God destroyed it (Gen 18:20). God only found **one** righteous man here, and that was Lot. He and his family were the only ones to be offered sanctuary.

Just a few generations later we read that Abraham's descendants were not living in the land that God had provided for them, and sent Moses to deliver them from their bondage in Egypt and bring them up into their Promised Land. God had made a covenant with Abraham, now he made another covenant, this time with Abraham's descendants through Isaac and Jacob. In this covenant which was declared to the people by Moses, God stated that he would be their God and they would be his people. However this people also rebelled and would not follow God's instructions which were given to them through Moses and so they condemned themselves to wander in the wilderness until they were all dead. (Num 14:28-30)

Throughout history God's people have continued to disregard his instructions. We read in the scriptures how God sent judges to his people to deliver them and get them back into his way. We also read about the prophets who were sent to guide them back into God's ways.

God's degree of correction for his children is like that of any father (Lev 26:15), it gets progressively more painful until they respond in the correct way, culminating in the fifth cycle of discipline by their removal from the land (Lev 26:27) as happened to Adam and Eve. When the disobedience of his children became so grievous that they would not follow his instructions God removed them altogether either into captivity as happened to both Judah and Israel or they were destroyed as happened to Sodom and Gomorrah and the whole world at the time of the Flood.

God had warned his children of the consequences of rebellion (Deu 28) so that they would not destroy the ongoing work of transforming the earth that he had created. God had finished his work but had then put his creation into the hands of man to develop under his instructions. As we should by now have realized, although God gave dominion of earth to mankind, he is still calling the shots. He as the great architect is still in charge, making sure that the development progresses in his way. When we understand this and stop kicking against the pricks as Saul of Tarsus had done (Act 9:5), and when we realize that it is futile to fight against God (Act 5:38-39), then the whole work can progress more smoothly.

A VOICE IN THE WILDERNESS

T he work of correction was especially needful for God's people when he sent John the Baptist to them. John was a man who was sent from God (Jn 1:6), he came as was prophesied of him as *a voice crying in the wilderness* to bear witness of Jesus as the Christ and to call the people to return to God as did Elijah in whose spirit he came (Mal 4:5-6; Mat 11:14-15). Although we read that he preached in the wilderness of Judea (Mt 3:1-3), he was not sent to preach in a natural wilderness but a spiritual wilderness. God's people had lost their way; they were living in their natural Promised Land but not their spiritual Promised Land, and for this reason they were not living in the blessings that God had made available to them through the covenant he had made with them, the Old Covenant, which the people had received and agreed through Moses. (Ex 19:5-8)

Today, many in the church are similarly not living in their spiritual Promised Land. They have entered into the New Covenant agreement with God which they received through Jesus, but like Israel of the Old Covenant, many are not living in the blessings that God has made available to them because of their disobedience. The blessings of God are for the obedient (Deu 28:1-2; 1Jn 3:22), not the disobedient (Deu 28:15). Through their disobedience, **all but two** of the adult population of Israel who entered into that Old Covenant with God perished in the wilderness without ever entering their Promised Land. The author of Hebrews warns those under the New Covenant not to make the same mistake (Heb 11:4, Num 14:22-23), and Jude reminds us that God destroyed those Israelites **after** he had saved them out of Egypt (Jude 1:5). This should be a sobering thought for those who believe that you cannot lose your salvation. (Heb 10:26-29)

If we review the history of Israel we will be able to see why it was necessary for God to send John the Baptist and why the people were failing to receive God's blessings.

Starting with Abraham we see that God blessed him for his obedience (Gen 22:15-18, 26:3-5) and made promises to his descendants (Gen 17:7-9). Paul writes about entering into those blessings by faith (Gal 3:9, 29), but Jesus elaborates and makes it quite clear that this faith entails **doing** the works of Abraham (Jn 8:39) which, as we have just read, is obedience to God.

Today there are those who say they believe or have faith but many are no different from those Jews who believed, and thought they would receive the inheritance just because they were Abraham's descendants. They were deceived, for without the obedience to God which Abraham had, they were marked as children of the devil, not sons of God. (Jn 8:31-44)

As the book of Hebrews tells us, Jesus didn't become the author of salvation to those that call him Lord, but to those who **obey** him (Heb 5:9). Obedience is implicit in biblical faith (Mt 7:21).

For us to expect to receive the blessings of God because we *say* we have received Jesus is quite presumptuous just like those Jews who believed (Jn 8:31). We become the sons of God by having the very nature of Christ formed in us

(Gal 4:19), then all of God's promises are available to us (2Cor 1:20). Obedience is the key to all of God's blessings, including entry to the kingdom of heaven, for obedience demonstrates love (Jn 14:21-24) and is the evidence of a transformed heart.

As we have seen, when God made his Old Covenant with Israel he promised them blessings for obedience and curses for disobedience (Deu 28:1-2, 15). It was never God's desire to curse his people, but he used this *carrot and stick* approach to encourage them to walk in his ways. All the time, God was drawing his people to himself. The problem that the people faced was that whilst their spirit was willing to follow God (Ex 19:5-8), their flesh was continually pulling them in the opposite direction. (Num 11:4-6)

We see how in the days of Abraham, Isaac and Jacob, they left the Land of Canaan which the Lord had said he would give them, because of a lack of bread, and went down into Gerar (Philistine country) and Egypt. God had to send Moses to deliver them from Egypt AND bring them up again into Canaan, a land flowing with milk and honey, God's Promised Land. (Ex 3:8, 17; 6:8)

Now Moses was a forerunner of Jesus (Deu 18:15-19). Moses delivered the people from Egypt because they could not free themselves, just as Jesus set us free from sin because we could not free ourselves. Moses showed them the way to the Promised Land, all they had to do was obey God's commands which he gave them through Moses and they would have walked into the Promised Land. Likewise, Jesus shows us *the way* into our Promised Land, all we have to do is obey God's commands which he gave us through Jesus and we will enter into our Promised Land, the kingdom of Heaven, for the true Promised Land is not a geographical location, it is a spiritual kingdom. We have seen how only two of the adult population who were delivered from Egypt came into the Promised Land; will it be an equally small proportion of those Jesus delivered who will enter heaven? (Mt 7:13-14)

Only the obedient will enter. (Mt 7:21)

In the deliverances of Moses and Jesus, you will notice a principle; God does not call us to do what we cannot do. What we could not do, he did for us through Moses and Jesus: that was his part. What we can do, he expects **us** to do; that is **our** part. Jesus has instructed us in *the way*, and said that those who hear his words AND keep them are wise (Mt 7:24). Obeying his instructions is our part.

When Peter was put in prison (Act 12:1-4) he was guarded by four quarternions of soldiers. Each quarternion would have responsibility for the prisoner for three hours, the night being divided into four periods of three hours. The quarternion consisted of four soldiers; it was usual for two to be chained to the prisoner and two to keep watch. This all took place within a locked and guarded prison.

Peter could not free himself so God sent an angel to deliver him: note what happens. The angel of the Lord struck him to wake him up and told him to get up. Peter didn't say 'I can't, I'm chained to these two guards'. He believed and as he got up the chains fell off – God did what Peter couldn't do as he obeyed. The angel told him to get dressed and follow him. He didn't help Peter this time because it was something Peter could do without help, Peter just had to be obedient. They passed the guards without being seen. Was Peter invisible, or did God close their eyes? They came to the prison gate which Peter couldn't open so it opened up all by itself. God did it for him, all Peter had to do was to be obedient and follow. Peter no longer needed help when he was free so the angel departed. (Act 12:7-11)

We read that when Moses was leading the Israelites to the Promised Land they were disobedient to God's commands, so although God had delivered them from Egypt he later destroyed them (Jude 1:5). Jude says this was because they did not believe, but if we look back at what this means we see that it was because of continued disobedience and murmuring. (Num 14:22-24)

What do you think will happen to those who have not believed Jesus (Jn 12:37), those who have heard but not obeyed (Mt 7:26-27)? God has already answered; their blood will be upon their own head, for he commanded them to listen and obey (Deu 18:18-19). Again, the author of Hebrews warns us that those who have heard and received the truth but continue to sin have rejected their salvation and only have judgment and the fires of hell awaiting them (Heb 10:26-29). Faith or belief without works is dead! (Jas 2:17-20)

Stephen recalled these days when he told the council that their fathers would not obey Moses, and in their hearts turned back to Egypt (Act 7:39). When they had nothing but manna to sustain them they remembered the fine food they had in Egypt (Num 11:4-6). The flesh is continually pulling us away from God and back into this world. If we yield to the flesh we will never enter our Promised Land.

Throughout the Old Testament we read how the Israelites continually disregarded God's instructions, and then, as a result of this disobedience they experienced the curses that God had promised would come upon them (Deu 28:15-68). When they had had enough, God sent them a deliverer, in the form of a Judge or when they were still in rebellion, a prophet to call them back into God's ways. Jesus told a story with the same pattern in the parable of the *Prodigal Son* (Lu 15:1-24) who, when he had had enough returned to his father's house.

We must remember that it is not God's will that any should perish, but that all should come to repentance. (Eze 33:11; 2Pe 3:9)

God always wants to restore his people to himself. We can see this clearly in the book of Joel when he says he will send his destroying army against his own people to bring them to repentance and afterwards he will restore the land, reversing the devastation that his army had brought (Joel 1:4, 2:25). We see how this principle was fulfilled when the first generation of Israelites to leave Egypt were destroyed, but the next generation, who were obedient to God, entered their Promised Land and were blessed. (Josh 21:43-45)

God is in the restoration business. Satan may have marred what God created, but that was only a temporary set-back. God's intention to populate this earth with mankind created in his image is still his will. He may have to let go of individuals or even whole nations or generations as with those disobedient Israelites, or the inhabitants of Sodom and Gomorrah or even the world in Noah's day, but if God didn't give up on mankind at the time of the Flood, he's not going to give up now. The earth **will** be filled with the glory of God as a showcase to the whole of creation. (Num 14:21)

In 787BC Amos wrote that a famine was coming; not a famine of bread but of hearing the words of the Lord (Amos 8:11). He lived in a period during which God had sent many prophets to turn his people back to his ways, starting with Elijah who had that great victory over the prophets of Baal on Mount Carmel about 906BC and turned the people back to God; and ending with Malachi who around 397BC prophesied that God would send Elijah again to turn the people back to him (Mal 4:5-6). After this time there were no more prophets declaring the word of God until John the Baptist was sent. Jesus declared that John fulfilled Malachi's prophecy (Mt 11:11-14). We refer to this period as the 400 years of silence; a famine of hearing the word of the Lord.

So we see that John the Baptist came as a voice crying in their spiritual wilderness to turn the people back to God immediately before Jesus came. John came in the spirit of Elijah whose return will herald the second coming.

One of the two witnesses of Revelation 11 clearly has the same anointing as Elijah, the other has the anointing of

Moses (Rev 11:5-6; 1Kin 17:1; 2Kin 1:10). These are the two who appeared with Jesus on the *Mount of Transfiguration*. (Mt 17:1-3)

This book echoes the voice of God crying to his people in **today's** wilderness, calling them back to himself. The defection to Baal had been so great in Elijah's day that he declared that he alone was left of God's prophets, the rest had been silenced; yet God told him that there was still a remnant of seven thousand that had not yielded to Baal. (1Kin 19:14, 18)

The defection to the world today is so bad that many Christians do not even realize that they have succumbed to the devil's temptations of the flesh and are not following the narrow *Way* that leads to life, but are on the broad way that leads to destruction (Mt 7:12-13). Yet there are many more who knowingly but secretly yield to such temptations whilst naming Jesus as their Lord and Saviour. They think they are getting away with what they are doing, but the only one who is getting away with anything is the devil – they are the ones being deceived.

The resurrection of life is for those who resist the deceptions of the devil (Rev 20:4-6) and follow Jesus along the narrow path. Remember Jesus' words when he said that in the last days, if it were possible even the very elect would be deceived. (Mt 24:24)

FOLLOWERS OF THE WAY

The disciples were first called Christians at Antioch (Act 11:26), they were previously known as *Followers of the Way.*

Jesus told the disciples that **he is** *the Way*, and that no one can come to the Father except by him (Jn 14:6).

The adherents of many religions are rightly purifying their spirits, and even if they are not natural Jews, by doing what is right they can become accepted by God (Rom 2:14-15, 27-29). They are making steps towards God. Access to heaven is open to all the gentile peoples of the world, but although some of them recognize Jesus as a great prophet, most have as yet failed to fully understand his role.

Jesus said that his words were not his own, but they were the words of his Father who told him what to say and speak (Jn 12:49-50). Jesus didn't do anything of his own accord, only those things the Father showed him to do (Jn 5:19). Again this emphasizes that it is God in heaven who is orchestrating the whole development of life on earth.

It was Father who spoke from heaven and said that Jesus was his beloved Son, in whom he was well pleased (why? – because of his obedience) and commanded us to listen to what Jesus had to tell us (Mt 17:5). God had spoken centuries earlier through Moses the deliverer saying that he would raise up a prophet like Moses who would speak the words that God gave him to speak, and that the people would have to face the consequences if they did not listen to what he had to tell them (Deu 18:18-19). We would therefore be wise to pay close attention to what Jesus said and the example of his life, for as Peter realized, he has the words of eternal life (Jn 6:68). His instruction is the **key** to the kingdom of heaven. Listen and obey.

Jesus plainly declares that he is the **only** *way* that man can reach heaven, but what exactly did he mean by this? Is Jesus *the person* the way to heaven, or did Jesus come to *show* us the way to heaven by his teaching and the personal example of his life? The answer is *both*.

Teaching in the church almost exclusively emphasizes Jesus *the person* as the way to heaven. The scriptures explain how he came, lived a sinless life and so was accepted by God as the spotless sacrifice required for sin, taking our place when he gave his life upon the cross. Being sinless, he was the only one who could pay the ransom for our souls. Nobody else ever has, or ever could pay the penalty for our sin, so without his death the penalty would have remained unpaid and we would all still be in our sin. Nobody could enter heaven because we are all tainted by the sins which have stained our lives (Rom 3:23, 6:23). Jesus was much more than the prophets who were sent before him; they were sent to lead the people back into God's way, but in addition to this Jesus also set us free from past sin by wiping the slate clean.

The **work** that Jesus was given to do by his Father was to be and to show the way for mankind, who had strayed from God's ways, to be re-united with the Father in heaven.

When Jesus stood by the well he told his disciples that he was sustained by doing the will of God and by finishing his work (Jn 4:34). When he died upon the cross he said '**It is finished**' (Jn 19:30). He had accomplished everything that **he** was given to do. Sadly, many people misconstrue these words and teach that **everything** is finished, when scripture quite clearly shows us that is not true. Just as Father finished his work and handed the work of creating more of mankind over to Adam before resting (Gen 2:2), so Jesus came to show the way and then handed the work of re-creation or spiritual rebirth over to his disciples, saying that they would do greater works than he had done because he was returning to the Father (Jn 14:12). He said to his Father that as he had been sent into the world, so he had sent them into the world (Jn 17:18) where they would continue being his witnesses (Act 1:8) right up to the end of the age (Mt 24:14). His work was finished but ours was just beginning, and like his Father, when he had finished his work, he sat down. (Heb 1:3)

On one occasion Jesus called the people to him and told them that anyone who would follow him to heaven must deny his own desires and take up his cross and emulate him (Mk 8:34). Luke tells us this is a perpetual daily activity, not a one-off experience. (Lu 9:23)

When the Wise Men came to Jesus they were guided by a bright star. It led them to Jesus, but they had to follow it to get to Jesus. Similarly, Jesus is like that bright star, leading us to Father, but we have to follow him to get to Father. Just as he heard his Father's voice and obeyed, so his sheep hear his voice and follow him. (Jn 10:27)

Jesus came into the world as the light of the world, shining in the darkness and showing the way out of darkness (Jn 12:46). He trained his disciples to follow him and to be light (Mt 5:14). To be delivered from the darkness of this world, the people must follow the light.

The scriptures declare that Jesus **is** the Word of God (Rev 19:13) and the psalmist writes that God's word is a lamp guiding our feet, and lighting our path (Psa 119:105). Man is incapable of finding his own way to God (Jer 10:23), he needs to be able to see God's way, and for that, others must be able to hear God's direction and show it to them.

The light is to show us the way out of darkness. The light shows the way that we need to walk in order to reach the Father. Isaiah says that whenever you turn to the right or to the left your ears shall hear a word behind you reminding you of the right way. (Isa 30:21)

Unless we follow the light we will walk in darkness and be as blind as the Pharisees of Jesus' day ending up in the ditch. (Mt 15:14)

Those Pharisees were not entering into the kingdom of heaven, and because of their wrong teaching and bad example they were preventing others from entering also. (Mt 23:13)

When it was time for Jesus to return to heaven he promised to send the Holy Spirit to continue to lead his followers (Jn 16:13-15) in the same way that a shepherd leads his sheep, and as we have just seen, those who are truly **his** sheep hear his voice and follow him. Paul writes that the true sons of God are those who follow the leading of the Spirit of God (Rom 8: 14). So, we see that Father leads and directs remotely, Jesus came to earth to lead in person, but now that he has returned to heaven the Holy Spirit has come to dwell in believers and lead from within. All the time God is leading his creation in the way that they must go, but it is only those who will obediently follow that will ever reach God in heaven.

Jacob dreamt and saw a ladder reaching from earth to heaven with the angels going up and down on it (Gen 28:12). This ladder was the way to and from heaven. Jesus told Nathanael that **he** (Jesus) was that ladder, saying that Nathanael would see the angels of God going up and down on him, the Son of man (Jn 1:51). Jesus also declared that he is the only way to the Father in heaven (Jn 14:6).

When we make a decision to become a Christian or a messianic believer we have taken our first step onto the bottom rung of that ladder. As we obey God's instructions more and more, so we climb higher and higher up the ladder.

Unless we climb all the way to the top by obeying God, we will never reach the kingdom of heaven. Jesus has provided the way and he has shown us that we must follow the way, but whether we reach our ultimate goal depends on how determined we are to dwell in His kingdom.

It is **our** responsibility to follow. Unless we follow in *the way* we will not become the sons of God and we will never come to the Father in heaven.

Jesus told his disciples that the Holy Spirit would be their teacher, instructing them in all things and reminding them of everything that he had told them (Jn 14:26) so that they would have a guide to follow.

The words of Jesus are of paramount importance to all who would enter the kingdom of Heaven, but much of the church has unwittingly replaced his teachings on the narrow way which leads to life (Mt 7:13-14) with a passive gospel which expects and requires nothing from the believer except *feigned* faith which is actually presumption.

Many say that salvation is all the grace of God, it is his free gift and there is nothing for us to do, making us passive participants. However, our salvation requires not a passive but a pro-active approach. Jesus said we must strive to enter in, for many will try and not be able (Lu 13:24). It is the violent who take the kingdom by force (Mt 11:12), and since the time of John the Baptist every man presses into the kingdom (Lu 16:16). We are encouraged to labour (Literally – *make haste*) to enter in (Heb 4:11) before the door is shut.

Rather than implying passivity, these scripture show us that an extremely pro-active approach is necessary. The laid-back Christian needs to wake up to reality before it is too late, for as we will see in the parable of *The Talents*, the servant who does nothing never enters the kingdom.

We should consider very carefully what Jesus had to say about those who would enter into the kingdom and those who would not. He told us that not everyone who refers to him as Lord will enter the kingdom of heaven, only those who **do** the will of his Father who is in heaven. He says that on the Day of Judgment many will say to him 'Lord, Lord, didn't we **prophesy** in your name? Didn't we **cast out demons** in your name? Didn't we **perform many miracles** all in your name?' But then he will say to them that he never knew them, telling these who live without regard to his law to depart from him. (Mt 7:21-23)

With these words Jesus makes it very clear that there will even be some who have been recognized as ministering **in his name** with **the gifts of the Spirit** that will not enter the kingdom of heaven. They have perhaps given their lives to the work of the ministry, but have not spent time on personal preparation. (1Cor 9:27; Php 3:13-14)

There is perhaps more to calling on the name of the Lord for salvation than many have attributed to the Prophecy of Joel (Joel 2:32) recorded in the book of Acts (Act 2:21), for there are many who profess to know God, but their actions and lack of obedience show that this is not true. (Tit 1:16; Jn 8:31-44)

At the beginning of his chapter on love to the Corinthian church, Paul gives a clue to the reason why many will be refused entry to the kingdom of God. He says that even though they may speak in tongues, prophesy, have knowledge and faith to move mountains; without love it is all meaningless for them as individuals, even though their gifts may benefit others. (1Cor 13:1-2)

Paul described the attitudes of many in the Corinthian church as carnal or worldly, which was evident through envy, strife and division (1Cor 3:1-3). These are not the characteristics of God so we must not emulate them, they are the characteristics of the world which is passing away (1Jn 2:15-18), yet they still persist in the church today. We should seek to attain a heart attitude of love and peace.

Jesus continued by telling a parable of *Two Houses* (Mt 7:24-27), one built on the rock, the other built on sand.

He said everyone that listens to what he says and acts upon his instructions by putting what he has told them into practice in their lives is like a wise man who builds his house on the rock. He said that no wind or rain or flood would be able to destroy that house because it was anchored on a sure and solid foundation, the rock which is Jesus, the word of God. But everyone that hears what he says and does not act upon his instructions is like a foolish man who builds his house on the sand which is of no use as a foundation because it is not solid and has nothing to bind it together, so under the force of wind the house has nothing firm to grip hold of and will be shifted. Under the force of water the sand foundation will be washed out causing the house to collapse catastrophically.

This parable tells of those who prepare themselves for entry into the kingdom of God and those who don't. Sadly there are many in the church who have not begun to prepare themselves because they say that they are saved by faith not by works, it is God's grace. They are presumptuously assuming that the work they must do has been done by Jesus – they are mistaken. It is this erroneous understanding of scripture that is leaving multitudes thinking they have salvation when they do not.

Obedience and love go hand in hand as the primary keys to the kingdom of heaven. This is why Jesus said to his disciples 'If you love me, obey my commandments' (Jn 14:15). He developed this link between obedience and love further by making clear that whoever receives his commandments and obeys them demonstrates his love, and that he and his Father will love such a person and live within them (Jn 14:21,23). To emphasize this point even more, he added that anyone who does not love him does not obey his commandments. He then set the seal of authority on what he had said by telling them that these words were not his, but were the words of his Father who sent him. (Jn 14: 24)

You need to pause right here and meditate on the significance of what God has just said to you through the scriptures.

To become followers of *The Way* we must hear and obey the principles that Jesus taught. For many Christians, his words go in one ear and out the other; it is like the seed that fell by the wayside in the parable of *The Sower*. They will never bear fruit because they will not change; they will not enter the kingdom of God even though they call Jesus 'Lord'. They will burn in the everlasting fire together with all who do not bear fruit. (Jn 15:1-6; Heb 6:7-8)

I once spoke with a sister who could not accept that God would send anyone to hell for disobedience, yet the Old Testament scriptures state this principal emphatically in the form of natural destruction (Deu 28:15-68). Jesus confirms this in the New Testament, saying that only those who obey God will enter the kingdom of heaven (Mt 7:21).

The people of Jesus' day were no different from the people of Isaiah's day and no different from so many Christians today. Jesus quoted Isaiah when he said of the Jews that they honour God by what they say, but their heart which is the important factor, is far removed from him; adding that their worship was a pointless waste of time because they taught and practiced doctrines and traditions which were nothing more than man made rules and regulations that made the commandments of God ineffective (Mt 15:3-9). He could just as easily have quoted the words that God spoke through Ezekiel when he said that the people come and hear his instructions but they will not obey them. They only show a love for God by what they say, but their heart follows their covetous desires (Eze 33:31). God says of these people that their thoughts are not his thoughts, and their ways are not his ways (Isa 55:8).

Unless **we** change **our** ways for God's ways we will not enter the kingdom of heaven, for if we are not in agreement or in unity with God in our thoughts and ways, we cannot live with him (Amos 3:3) and will be separated from him throughout eternity.

God spoke through Isaiah likening his children, the Jewish rulers and people, to those of Sodom and Gomorrah whom he destroyed (Isa 1:10-20). He told them that even though their sacrifices were in accordance with the law they were unacceptable, and other practices that were also in accordance with the law were a waste of time **because their hearts were unchanged**. He said he would not listen to their prayers until they made themselves clean on the inside which would be evident through works of righteousness (v.17). On another occasion he told them that punishing their flesh through fasting was also a waste of time because their hearts were not in agreement with his (Isa 58:5). He told them that the kind of fast he would find acceptable was doing works of righteousness (vv.6-7), and that then and only then would he hear and answer their prayers (vv.8-11).

Whether it is Old or New Testament makes no difference, the principles and heart of God are the same in both. He never changes.

THE PARABLES OF JESUS

Having established the authority and importance of Jesus' words, let us turn our attention to his teaching.

After he had answered his disciples' questions on when the destruction of the temple and the end of the age will come by giving them the signs that would indicate these times, Jesus warned his disciples to watch (Mt 24:42) and be ready (Mt 24:44) and told them of the dire consequences for those of **his servants** who fail to make themselves ready by obeying his commands in his parable of *The Faithful and the Evil Servants* (Mt 24:45-51). The final verse tells us that the evil servants will be severed in the same way that you might amputate a diseased limb or cut out a cancer, and sent to a place with the hypocrites.

Jesus had repeatedly referred to the scribes and Pharisees as hypocrites (Mt 23:13-29) and in another place added that unless our righteousness exceeds that of the scribes and Pharisees we will not enter the kingdom of heaven (Mt5:20). He then went on to give them graphic illustrations in the form of three further parables to distinguish between those who would be ready and therefore fit for the kingdom of heaven and those who would not.

Matthew 25 records these three parables, the first being the parable of *The Ten Virgins* (Mt 25:1-13).

This parable tells the story of those who are ready at his coming and those who are not. Jesus' preliminary instruction had been *to watch*. He had just given all the signs so that those who are alive at his coming would be able to recognize the times as they approached, but we find these ten virgins, who are **all** waiting expectantly for the bridegroom, are asleep until they hear a voice crying out 'behold the bridegroom is coming', they are not watching. What does it mean to be *asleep*? Their spiritual eyes are closed, they do not know what God is doing, yet God does nothing without first revealing it to his servants the prophets (Amos 3:7). They would fit into the same category as those religious leaders who were asleep at his first coming (Mt 16:1-3). They would have already heard a voice crying in the wilderness saying 'The kingdom is at hand, prepare the way of the Lord, make his paths straight' (Mt 3:2-3). They are not watching! It is only as they wake up and trim their lamps that the foolish virgins realize their lack. They have not heeded the warning. They have no oil in their lamps. They are not ready. They are too late!

We read that five were wise and five were foolish. Jesus tells us in the parable of *The Two Houses* (Mt 7:24-27) that the wise are those who hear his words **and** obey them. When he says to watch he is not giving an option, he is giving an instruction; he means that we should look out for the signs, not be spiritually asleep. Those who hear his words and do not take heed he calls foolish. It is as we take note of what Jesus says and do it that we find ourselves following *The Way* that leads to life. His words are instruction in righteousness (2Tim 3:16) and lead to works of righteousness as we follow them.

It is works of righteousness that John the Baptist was looking for in the Pharisees and Sadducees that would demonstrate changed lives (Mt 3:8) and would show they were fit to enter the kingdom of heaven. Jesus confirmed that righteousness is the indicator by which we are judged fit to enter the kingdom of heaven (Mt 5:20). This is the fruit that Jesus was looking for on the fig tree, both in actuality (Mt 21:18-19) and in parables (Lu 13:6-9). It is the works of righteousness that demonstrate changed hearts and therefore true faith. James pointed out this truth when he wrote that faith without works is dead (Jas 2:20), and in the same way, the lamp without oil is dead, it gives no light. What good is a lamp if it gives no light? It is like the salt that has lost its effectiveness (Mt 5:13-16), it is good for nothing. Is it any surprise that the five foolish virgins who had no oil in their lamps were shut out of the kingdom? Those Christians who do not follow Jesus by obeying his words are like the Pharisees; their lives do not manifest the fruit of the Spirit in general and righteousness in particular (Gal 5:22) and therefore they have no works of righteousness to show.

John writes that all who do acts of righteousness are born of God (1Jn 2:29) and whoever does not do acts of righteousness is not of God (1Jn 3:10). It is righteousness that is the wedding garment of the saints (Rev 19:7-8), and as we have seen, it is the bride's responsibility to dress and make herself ready for the wedding. This is separate to the finished work of Christ on the cross.

The Pharisees tried to make themselves appear righteous on the outside, but Jesus called them hypocrites (Mt 23:27-28); for God does not judge by the outward appearance, but by the heart of man (1Sam 16:7). It is our heart or spirit that will be judged (Mt 5:28). When our body dies it decays and reverts to dust, but our spirit returns to God who gave it (Ecl 12:7). He will then be looking for a reflection of himself when he looks at our spirit. When our heart has been transformed into the image of God, then God's Spirit will witness with our spirit that we are indeed the sons of God (Rom 8:16).

All ten of these virgins expect to be received by the bridegroom but five will be devastated when they are rejected because they have not made themselves ready; they have not changed inside. They may not be wearing a worldly Babylonish garment like Achan (Josh 7:20-21), but a garment of hypocrisy like those of the Pharisees is equally as bad. Neither is acceptable, our spirit must be clothed in the wedding garment of righteousness.

This requirement is further clarified by Jesus' parable of *The Marriage of the King's Son* (Mt 22:1-14). In this story we read how those who were originally invited would not even come to the wedding, a picture of those Jews who rejected Jesus, but then the king told his servants to call all they could find to the wedding. This is where the gentiles receive their invitation (Mt 8:11-12). There is however a man who has been called and has come expectantly to the wedding but is not wearing a wedding garment, he is not clothed in righteousness, so he is cast out.

It is said that in the eastern tradition the bridegroom provided the garments for his guests. Jesus made it possible for everybody to be clothed in righteousness through his death on the cross; we all have the power to become the sons of God through obedience (Jn 1:12). Isaiah was obedient and was therefore able to greatly rejoice in the Lord and said his soul would be joyful in his God, because God had clothed him with the garments of salvation, he had covered him with the robe of righteousness, in the same way that a bridegroom covers himself with ornaments, and as a bride embellishes herself with her jewels (Isa 61:10).

This man who had been invited is one of the foolish virgins, he had not changed into his wedding garment, his robe of righteousness. Jesus concludes this parable by saying that many are called but few are chosen. There are multitudes who, like this man, are waiting for the coming of the Lord, but have not made themselves ready.

Peter said that to make sure we are both called **and** chosen we should add seven godly characteristics to our faith so that we should not fall, and so that an entrance would be made for us into the everlasting kingdom (2Pet 1:4-11). These seven characteristics are not exhaustive, but they are typical of the character traits of God that Paul refers to as the fruit of the Spirit. It is those who follow the leading of the Spirit so that they develop and manifest the fruit of the Spirit in their lives who will enter the kingdom. Those whose lives exhibit the works of the flesh will never enter the kingdom (Gal 5:19-24). As we have seen, unless we manifest the fruit of righteousness we will burn in hell fire (Mt 3:10; Jn 15:1-8) even if we do call ourselves *Christians*.

We see that the five wise virgins who had made themselves ready, go in with Jesus and the door is then shut. The foolish try hastily to get oil for their lamps and knock on the door to be let in, but Jesus tells them **I DON'T KNOW YOU**, I don't recognize myself in you. Some people mistakenly interpret these words to suggest that these foolish virgins only miss the wedding supper and later, perhaps after the tribulation are permitted to enter, but Jesus warns us to strive to enter in at the narrow gate, for many will try to enter in and will not be able. (Lu 13:24). When the door is shut, it is SHUT!

Don't waste precious time, start getting ready now. Be dressed and ready, with your lights burning; and be like servants that are looking diligently for their lord to return from the wedding; so that when he comes and knocks, they may open the door to him immediately (Lu 12:35-36). The word *burning* which is used here means *set on fire*, these are not passive lukewarm Christians. Those Christians who are only lukewarm will be spewed out (Rev 3:16). So called 'carnal Christians' will not make it unless they change.

The second parable of Matthew 25 is the parable of *The Talents.* (Mt 25:14 -30)

This parable tells the story of a man who put everything he had in the hands of his servants before going away. We read that two of these servants used these *talents* that they had been given and produced an increase, but the third did nothing except keep his talent in a safe place. When the lord of these servants returned he was pleased with the first two servants and ushered them into his kingdom, but he was very angry with the third, and called him a lazy servant. This servant was cast out of his presence.

This parable is a picture of Jesus empowering **his** disciples (servants) and returning to heaven; then at his second coming judging who had obeyed his commands by their work in the kingdom to produce an increase, and therefore who was fit for heaven and who was not.

The fate of the lazy servant was to be cast into outer darkness. Now if we bear in mind that God is light and in him there is **no darkness at all** (1Jn 1:5) it becomes clear that this servant does not enter heaven, but spends eternity as far away from God as possible, for he is cast into *outer* darkness, the same fate as those who rejected his wedding invitation (Mt 8:11-12).

It was God's original commission that man should be fruitful and multiply (Gen 1:28). After the Flood of Noah's time, God repeated this instruction (Gen 9:1). God didn't change his plans just because of Satan's intervention which caused him to start again.

As mankind began to multiply again, we see that the world split into two camps just as Israel did when ten of the twelve tribes rebelled against king Rehoboam son of Solomon (1Kin 12:16-20). Some chose to follow God, others Baal, typified by Babylon which always represents rebellion against God.

God gave Nebuchadnezzar the king of Babylon a dream in which he showed him that the kingdoms of this world which emanated from Babylon and had the same spirit would be destroyed, but the followers of God would multiply and fill the whole world (Dan 2:31–45). This victorious kingdom is the one established by Jesus, so it is his followers who are to multiply.

Before Jesus returned to heaven he promised to send the Holy Spirit (the gifts of the Spirit are represented by the talents in the parable) to empower his disciples, and commissioned them to go into all the world and preach the gospel (Mt 28:19). This was to be the means of multiplying the church, which we see grew by 3,000 on the day of Pentecost following Peter's preaching (Act 2:41). This commission is the same one that God gave to Adam and Eve, and to Noah and his family, except that now the physical multiplication of God's kingdom is achieved not by natural birth but by spiritual rebirth. This spiritual transformation is achieved by the heart or spirit of man being born again.

After personal transformation, this work of preaching the gospel to obtain converts who are then to be discipled (Mt 28:20) is the second most important function of the church as a whole, and individuals in particular, for the husbandman is to partake of the fruit first. (2Tim 2:6)

Jesus discipled the twelve to become like him and continue the work. They were to become followers of the way. They in turn were to do the same; to disciple converts to be like Jesus and follow in the way. Jesus said that anyone who did not forsake all that he had could not be his disciple (Lu 14:33). The prerequisite for becoming a disciple of Jesus is to give up everything of the old life in the natural world just as those first disciples did. You cannot serve God and mammon. (Mt 6:24)

Just as the man in the parable gave talents to all his servants, so Jesus gave his followers the Holy Spirit with abilities or gifts for all who receive him (1Cor 12:7). Firstly this empowering was given to the twelve (Lu 9:1-2), then to the seventy (Lu 10:1-9), then to all his servants (Act 2:38-39) and will remain in operation until our work is completed (Mt 24:14) – then Jesus will return.

The servants in the parable were expected to continue the work of increasing their lord's estate, and as we have already seen, Jesus told his disciples that they would do greater works than he had done because he was returning to heaven (Jn 14:12). Jesus had spoken to his Father saying that he had sent his disciples out into the world just like Father had sent him into the world (Jn 17:18), so that they could continue the work of transforming the world and fulfilling God's original plan by eradicating the corruption that Satan had started in the Garden of Eden. They were to continue this work empowered by the Spirit until his return (Mt 24:14).

God, who we will remember is orchestrating all activity on earth, planned for the work to proceed in an ordered way. Ministry gifts were given to men in order to prepare and train up those who receive the gospel for the work of the ministry (Eph 4:11-16). It was to be like a self-perpetuating conveyor belt of activity.

Like the servants in the parable, we are only of use to the work of the kingdom if we do what we have been called to do. What do you think the boss with total overall control will do with those of his workers who will not work?

Jesus told a parable of *Two sons* (Mt 21:28-32) who were called by their father to go into his vineyard to work. Although this parable was probably aimed more precisely at personal transformation, the principle reveals that if we do not obey, we are not doing Father's will, and Jesus warned that only those who actively **do** Father's will enter the kingdom of heaven (Mt 7:21), this is why a wise man hears and obeys (Mt 7:24) otherwise he is just deceiving himself (Jas 1:22).

Jesus told his disciples that they were the salt of the earth, but added that the salt is of no use if it is ineffective and will be discarded. He said they were the light of the world, but that the light is of no use unless it is allowed to shine in the darkness for all to see (Mt 5:13-16).

Even though we don't deserve the kingdom of heaven, it is the gift of God that makes it freely available to those who want it and will meet the entry conditions. However, there will be no freeloaders in heaven, contrary to some popular teaching; so be warned, you have to work out your own salvation with fear and trembling (Php 2:12).

Hear another warning that Jesus gives. When Jesus sent out his twelve disciples he told them that they would face opposition and would suffer (Mt 10:16-25). In spite of this, he warned them of the consequences of failing to do the work of preaching the gospel which he had given them to do. He told them not to fear what man might do to them, but to declare openly what he had instructed them privately, and concluded by saying that they should be less concerned about losing their lives, than having their body and soul cast into hell fire by God if they failed to obey him through fear (Mt 10:26-28). He who seeks to save his life shall lose it (Mt 16:25). It was this same fear that caused the Israelites to disobey God when they were told to go into the Promised Land and take it (Num 13:26-33). They saw the high walled cities and the giants and were afraid; as a result they never entered their Promised Land. The author of Hebrews warns the church not to make the same mistake (Heb 4:1-2) which was failure to obey God.

It is the same principle as being in the armed forces in a war. To gain the victory some will lose their lives, but these are only our physical lives which will be over in the blink of an eye. It is only the eternal state which is of any real consequence. The people of the kingdom established by Jesus are assured of the ultimate victory, for Jesus said that the gates of hell would not prevail against the church (Mt 16:18), and in addition to Nebuchadnezzar's dream in which God told him that the kingdoms of this world would be destroyed, but the kingdom of Christ would be everlasting (Dan 2:34-35, 44), Daniel tells us that judgment will be given in favour of the saints of the most high (Dan 7:18, 22, 27).

The third and final parable of Matthew 25 is the parable of *The Sheep and Goats* (Mt 25:31-46)

This parable tells the story of Jesus at his second coming sitting on the throne and gathering all nations before him. It tells us that he will separate them into two groups in the same way that a shepherd divides the sheep from the goats. Now the variety of sheep and goats which are a common sight in the UK appear very different from each other, but some breeds in the Middle East are almost indistinguishable. He does not separate them according to their *appearance*, but according to their *works of righteousness*, (Mt 7:15-16) it's the only way to be certain.

Only the *righteous* sheep will be permitted to enter the kingdom of heaven, the *unrighteous* goats are sent away into everlasting fire. There will be no wolves (or goats) masquerading in sheep's clothing entering the kingdom of heaven no matter how well they dress themselves up, for Jesus will only gather those bearing fruit into his kingdom (Mt 3:11-12), the rest have an appointment with the fire.

This is why John the Baptist warned the Pharisees and Sadducees of their need to bear fruit (Mt 3:7-8) when he called them *vipers*, a term also used by Jesus of the scribes and Pharisees when he called them serpents, saying they were a generation of vipers and asked them how they expected to escape the damnation of hell (Mt 23:33). He had told others that they were in fact children of the devil (Jn 8:44) who is also known as the dragon and the serpent (Rev 20:2).

Why do we suppose Jesus taught so much about the need to bear fruit? It is because those who don't bear fruit end up as fuel for the lake of fire. (Jn 15:1-8)

Jesus describes the sheep as those who have responded with love and compassion to the needs of their brothers and sisters. They have done to others as they would have others do to them if their situations were reversed (Mt 7:12).

He says that whatever they have done to one another, they have done to him. Those that failed to act in this way lacked love and compassion, and thereby identified themselves as goats rather than sheep. In the parable both the sheep and the goats called Jesus 'Lord', but the goats did not expect to be examined in this way, implying that if they had seen Jesus in need they would have helped him. These goats may have looked like the sheep outwardly, but inwardly they lacked the characteristics of sheep, and like the five foolish virgins who outwardly looked just like the wise virgins, they were not ready, they had not been transformed (Rom 12:2). Just as the foolish virgins had no oil, so these goats had no fruit or works of righteousness.

This third parable deals with the evidence of those who are truly reborn in the image of God. They demonstrate that they are ready like the wise virgins by their fruit or works of righteousness.

Let us understand that the law as a set of rules and regulations will not save us. We don't become the finished article by simply following a set of instructions; it's not like painting by numbers. To pay lip service to the law as the scribes and Pharisees did is only superficial, it is the changed heart which results in and from obedience that saves us, even though this will encompass keeping God's standards as expressed in the law. The changed heart will be one that manifests the same characteristics as God – the fruit of the Spirit. If we continue in Jesus' *way* by obeying his words, then this change will occur, and the result will be our desire to do the things that God would do, these are the works of righteousness that identify a changed heart.

The psalmist writes of his delight to do the will of God, adding that God's law is written in his heart. (Psa 40:8)

It is the good works of love and compassion in the parable that distinguish the sheep from the goats.

When Jesus dictated letters to the seven churches of Asia, he started each letter with the words *I know your works*, and ended every letter with the words *He that has an ear to hear, let him hear what the Spirit says to the churches*. Jesus tells five of the seven **churches** that their **works** are unacceptable and calls them to repent or face the consequences. He tells them to repent out of his love for them and his desire to see them transformed into what the church should be. Sadly, if he were to dictate letters of correction and send them to church leaders today, some of them would take offense instead of receiving correction with joy (Heb 12:5-11). How many churches do you suppose he is calling to repentance today? If only they have ears to hear!

So then, the parable of *The Ten Virgins* shows us the need to be ready if we expect to enter the kingdom of heaven, *The Talents* shows us the need to produce an increase in terms of multiplication by doing the work of the kingdom, and *The Sheep and Goats* shows us the need for personal transformation in terms of fruit in our own lives. Vessels that do not come up to the potter's standard go into the fire. One certain way that Christians can ensure that they are refused entry to the kingdom of God is to do nothing. The foolish virgins did not make themselves ready, they did not fill their lamps with oil; the servant with one talent did nothing with the ability his lord had given him; and the goats did nothing to help those in need. Many Christians are passive and do nothing once they become Christians.

Jesus also told the parable of *The Tares* (Mt 13:24-30, 36-43) in which Dean Trench asserts in his *Notes on the Parables of our Lord* that the tares are not an easily identifiable weed, but rather a bastard wheat which is only distinguishable from genuine wheat at the time that the fruit appears, and hence Jesus' statement that they shall be known by their fruits (Mt 7:15-20), not by what they call themselves, not by how they look, not by their ministry or spiritual gifts – but by their fruit.

The end of the tares is the same as the end of all that do not bear good fruit; it is to be burned in the lake of fire. Until the fruit appears, the tares look similar to the good wheat, just as the sheep and goats and the wise and foolish virgins appear similar.

Paul writes to Timothy that pure religion is to help the fatherless and widows in their distress. Without a father or husband to bring home the food, the children would often be forced to resort to theft, and the widows to prostitution in order to survive.

When we look at the early church, we see that they understood the need to help one another. They sold their possessions and distributed the proceeds to those amongst them that had need (Act 2:44-46; 4:34).

Jesus told his disciples to love one another because in the act of love they would demonstrate to the world that they were truly like Jesus - **his** disciples (Jn 13:34-35). John asks how the love of God can dwell in a brother or sister who has the ability to help his fellow believers that are in need yet does not do so (1Jn 3:17), thus linking this caring, compassionate characteristic to love.

Let us move on to consider other parables. Some consider *The Rich Man and Lazarus* (Lu 16:19-31) to be a story rather than a parable because it mentions the name of the beggar; we should not be concerned with what it is called, but what it teaches us. In this story we have two people, a rich man who wears fine clothes and eats abundantly every day, and a beggar named Lazarus who sits at the rich man's gate craving even the crumbs that fall from his table. Both of them die and find their positions are reversed. After death the rich man finds himself in the torment of hell fire, and Lazarus is with Abraham.

The rich man saw Lazarus and had the ability to help him, but did nothing to help him. The love of God was not in his heart (1Jn 3:17). The sin of the rich man was not that he had riches, but that he consumed his wealth on his own lusts and did not have compassion for his neighbour. What is the second greatest commandment in the law? Love your neighbour **as yourself** (Mt 22:39). This is not an option, it is a command. You cannot command an emotion. Godly love is not an emotion, it is an act of your will.

Those who live in what we call the developed or industrialized countries are amongst the richest in the world, even though most do not recognize this fact because they compare themselves with others in their own country or peer group rather than with the rest of humanity. Does Jesus see you as a rich man in terms of the resources of this world? Here is a guide for you – if you have more than you **need** to survive on a daily basis, then you are rich in the materialism of this world, but may well be poor in spiritual wealth (Rev 3:17-19; Mat 6:19-21).

The **average** personal worldly income is about £680/year, with 80% of the world living on less than about £2250/year. You might say that you couldn't possibly live on £680/year – well how do you think half the world's population feels? How rich are **you** towards God in sharing what he has given you with him (others)? Jesus said it is hard for a rich man to enter the kingdom of heaven, it is easier for a camel to go through the eye of a needle (Mt 19:23-24; Lu 6:24). He pronounces woes upon rich people saying they have had their blessings (Lu 6:24). The kingdom of heaven is reserved for the poor (Lu 6:20; Jas 2:5) like Lazarus.

Contrast this parable with *The Good Samaritan* (Lu 10:30-37). In this story, A Jew is on a journey when he is set upon by thieves and left badly injured. A priest and a Levite pass by and don't help him, but a Samaritan comes and does everything in his power to help the man. The Samaritans and Jews were not considered particularly friendly neigh-bours, in fact the Jews referred to them as dogs (Jn 4:9), so the Samaritan might have thought that this Jew wasn't his responsibility, but Jesus asked which of the three it was that had acted as a neighbour to the injured man, to which a lawyer answered that he who helped the injured Jew was his neighbour. Jesus then instructed him to **go and do the same**. The Samaritan had a heart of compassion, unlike the priest and Levite, and helped this Jew who was in need and could not help himself.

Consider how Jesus might view a Muslim who similarly helps a Jew, or vice versa. God looks on the heart, not the outward appearance.

By their actions (or lack of them), the *Rich Man* showed himself to be a *goat*, but the *Samaritan* showed himself to be one of the *sheep*.

Consider the parable of ***The Rich Fool*** (Lu 12:16-21). In this story a rich man had a bumper harvest. He decided to build bigger barns in which to store his crops and to live a life of ease, eating, drinking and having a good time; but God called him a fool for he was not rich towards God.

This fool was happy because of his windfall, but he was not thankful, and decided to consume his fortune on his own lusts and pleasures like the *Rich Man*. He did not consider that God had given him an increase so that he could use it to help others, so he was not rich toward God, and that night he died, leaving all his goods behind for others – it was then too late for him to repent. This parable was spoken in response to a man who wanted some of his brother's inheritance. Those who are covetous of riches will not inherit the kingdom.

Consider the parable of ***The Unmerciful Servant*** (Mt 18:23-35). In this story a servant owed his master so much money that when he was asked to repay this debt he could not, but when the servant asked his master to give him more time the master forgave all his debt. This same servant went and found another servant and told him to repay the small amount that he owed him, but when this second servant could not pay, the first servant had him thrown in prison. When this came to the attention of their master, he was angry and said to the first servant that he should have had compassion on his fellow servant and forgiven the debt even as his master had forgiven him. Furthermore, he told him that because he had not forgiven, he would have his own forgiveness rescinded and would go to prison until he had paid all his debt. Jesus said that his heavenly Father will deal with each of us in the same way; we will not receive forgiveness from God for our sin if we do not forgive our brother's transgression against us **from our hearts**, because it shows that we haven't been transformed.

Forgiveness is freely available to us just as it was to this first servant, but unless we exhibit the same compassion and forgiveness as God to our brother, then we will not be forgiven ourselves. Quite often we harbour deep hurts and find it difficult to truly forgive the one who caused those hurts. For many, it's not that they **can't** forgive, but that they **won't**. This marks their hearts as being incompatible with God, and therefore unfit for his kingdom.

The eternal consequences of failing to forgive are catastrophic, so work on it now. Do something good or positive for anyone who has wounded your spirit; bridge the gap to heal the wound. Divorced husbands and wives especially take note!

All of these parables that Jesus told are for you to understand that there are many who will not be able to enter the kingdom of heaven because they have failed *the heart test*. Make sure you are ready!

WHAT IS THE PURPOSE OF LIFE?

Having read the previous chapter it should not be difficult to realize that life is a window of opportunity for your spirit to be transformed from a selfish to a selfless condition; to become once again compatible with your creator by putting away the desires and temptations of your flesh which Satan makes enticing, just as he did with Adam and Eve, and developing the character traits of God's Spirit, so that you might become fit to spend eternity with Him in His kingdom.

There are many zealous servants of all religions who are convinced they are doing God's will through acts of destruction and murder but they are mistaken. There were some believing Jews who sought to Kill Jesus because his teachings did not agree with their own understanding. They thought that God was their Father, but Jesus corrected them, saying that they were in fact **children of the devil** (Jn 8:31-47). Doesn't this sound just the same as many religious extremists today?

When the intolerant extremists of religion cannot persuade others to follow their ideology, they have historically resorted to intimidation, violence and murder – all in the name of their religion. Yet quite clearly, such aggression is incompatible with the love, compassion and mercy which they claim to represent. This physical aggression has mainly been directed at those of other religions or other sects within their own religion with whom these protagonists find themselves in ideological conflict; yet the adherents of religion are all seeking for the one true God, even if they are in some areas misguided in their understanding of exactly what is required of them or how to achieve it.

Jesus told his followers that it is better to love our enemies than to hate them (Mt 5:43-45). He said that he had come to bring abundant life, but that the enemy of our souls had come to steal, kill and destroy (Jn 10:10).

He also taught that a house divided against itself cannot stand (Mk 3:25), so it should come as no surprise that the devil will employ tactics of division amongst those seeking God. Even amongst those who have not been deceived by Satan into thinking that violence is the way forward, there are still many that regard others within their own faith with suspicion and remain separated from them. Scripture is quite clear that there is power in unity, whether it is for good or evil (Lev 26:8; Deu 32:30). God used this principle of division at Babel against those who were in unity (Gen 11:6).

Anyone who thinks that God who seeks love, compassion and mercy in his children would sanction hatred, intimidation and violence from them as a means to achieve this has been completely deceived, for these represent two opposing hearts.

Paul tells us that the natural precedes the spiritual (1Cor 15:46). Much of the Old Testament deals with what is natural so that we might understand the spiritual truth that it portrays. Circumcision of the flesh points us to circumcision of the heart (Rom 2:28-29), a physical action pointing to a spiritual one. In the Old Testament God often called for destructive physical action so that we may understand that our enemy must be completely annihilated, but our battle is not a physical one with those of other religious beliefs, our battle is a spiritual one (Eph 6:12). Our battle is primarily within ourselves, it is **our** spirit that fights against **our** flesh (Gal 5:17). Our battle is against the deceptions and temptations of the devil **in our own lives**; it is spiritual. The battleground is our mind.

Jesus did not condone the actions of the woman who was caught in the act of adultery, but shamed those who wanted to kill her by getting them to focus on the sin **in their own lives** (Jn 8:2-11). When we have removed the plank from our own eye, we will understand more clearly and be able to help one another rather than destroy each other (Lu 6:41-42). Religious extremists of whatever persuasion would do well to realize this.

HEARING HIS VOICE and SEEING HIS KINGDOM

Paul writes that we do not see the kingdom of God clearly, but as it were through the reflection in a mirror having an opaque or smoked glass surface, so we don't see it clearly, but we do see in part (1Cor 13:12). The degree to which we see it depends on the development of our spiritual eyesight, for the kingdom of God is not seen through natural eyes but spiritual ones, and it is revealed to us by the Spirit of God. (1Cor 2:9-10)

We can clearly see this world through our natural eyes, its effects are all around us, but God has given us his Spirit so that we might see his kingdom (1Cor 2:12).

We are a triune being - spirit, soul and body. Our natural mind is incapable of receiving and understanding information pertaining to the kingdom of God because it can only be discerned spiritually (1Cor 2:14).

Our body or flesh receives information concerning the natural world through our five natural senses. It can only distinguish between likes and dislikes; it has no ability to distinguish between right and wrong. Our spirit however is the converse; it has no ability to function as a receptor of likes and dislikes, only between right and wrong through hearing God. The functions of the body and the spirit are diametrically opposed to one another. They have different functions and operate in different realms.

As a poor analogy, we could compare natural sight with seeing through night vision glasses. On a pitch black night we cannot see by natural vision, but we can see if we have night vision glasses which operate not in the visible spectrum of light, but in the infra-red spectrum which is invisible to natural sight.

When Jesus was asked by the Pharisees when the kingdom of God should appear, he told them that it's appearing cannot be seen with the natural eyes, for it is not a natural kingdom but a spiritual one (Lu 17:20). The Pharisees expected the kingdom to be established in a particular physical place, but Jesus told them that the kingdom of God is within us (Lu 17:21).

Mankind experiences the world around him the only way he can, through the natural senses, but he cannot see the kingdom of God for it is spiritually discerned. This is why Jesus could not speak to men directly about the kingdom of heaven, but had to speak to them in parables - stories of natural occurrences to portray spiritual truths; but without spiritual eyes and ears they still could not understand these parables unless they were explained.

Jesus spoke with Nicodemus, one of the religious leaders responsible for showing the people the way into the kingdom of God. He told him that unless a man is born again he cannot see the kingdom of heaven (Jn 3:3), but this was beyond Nicodemus' comprehension; he could not visualize how he could return into his mother's womb and be born again (Jn 3:4). Jesus had to explain that he was not talking about natural birth but spiritual birth, saying that what is born of the spirit is spirit and what is born of the flesh is flesh (Jn 3:6). The spiritual and natural do not mix, they exist in different realms, but in the same place at the same time.

As spiritual leaders it was essential that the Pharisees should be able to see and understand spiritual matters, yet they could not. How then could they possibly lead people into a spiritual kingdom that they themselves could not see? They could not. Jesus called them blind leaders of the blind, concluding that they would not be able to follow the path and both they and those who followed them would fall into the ditch (Mt 15:14).

The disciples asked Jesus why he did not speak plainly about the kingdom of heaven, but in parables, to which he replied that not everybody had been given the right to know the mysteries of the kingdom of heaven (Mt 13:10-11).

When God's chosen people, the Israelites had repeatedly ignored his covenant with them and would not obey his commandments, he sent them prophets to remind them of his ways, but they would not obey (Jer 35:15; 44:15-17), and instead they mistreated and often killed them (Mt 23:34-35). As a direct result, God said that they would no longer be able to hear his voice; they would cease to get guidance from heaven (Amos 8:11).

Up until the time Jesus was born there had been 400 years of silence from heaven since the last prophet had been sent; the religious leaders had been unable to hear the voice of God and were continually looking for a sign from heaven (1Cor 1:22).

The Pharisees and Sadducees came to Jesus asking him to show them a sign from heaven, but he replied that they were only capable of understanding the signs of natural events like the weather and said that they would receive no sign except that of the prophet Jonas because of the evil condition of their hearts. (Mt 16:1-4)

We see this same inability to hear from heaven back in the time of Eli the priest.

We read that the word of the Lord was precious in those days because there was no open vision (1Sam 3:1). Now we know that where there is no vision the people perish (Pr 29:18). Without God's direction for mankind the people are lost, for mankind is incapable of directing his own way (Jer 10:23), he becomes as spiritually blind as the Pharisees.

Eli had not been obedient to God (1Sam 3:13-14) and as a result his ability to see spiritually (as well as naturally) had faded (1Sam 3:2). He had made an incorrect flesh judgement against Hannah (1Sam 1:9-14). The lamp of God in the temple, which represented the word of God to direct their way (Psa 119:105) was never to be extinguished, it was to burn continually (Ex 27:20), and yet it was going out.

The religious leaders of Jesus' day could not hear God because their minds were cluttered with natural things, and because they could not hear his voice they had substituted their own ways for his - traditions that made the word of God ineffective. (Mt 15:3-6)

The voice of Isaiah had cried out centuries before calling the people to forsake their ways and thoughts and return to God's ways and to have his mind, because man's ways and thoughts are nothing like his. (Isa 55:7-8)

Jesus quoted Isaiah when he said that the people of his day honoured God by what they said, but their hearts were not in tune with his at all, which resulted in their worship being completely pointless because they taught man's doctrines. (Mt 15:8-9) Their lives were not in agreement with the words they uttered.

If we cannot hear God's voice we cannot see his kingdom and our religion is a pointless deception.

DEVELOPING SPIRITUAL EYES AND EARS

You don't suddenly get spiritual eyes and ears any more than you can suddenly understand or speak a foreign language, or any more than you can plant the seed of a fruit tree today and expect instant fruit. I once had a friend and work colleague who said he would become a Christian when he saw the mark of the beast being implemented (Rev 13:16), but by then it will be too late, for as John the Baptist warned, everyone who does not bear good fruit will end in the fire (Mt 3:10), and fruit takes time to develop and grow.

When Jesus was training his disciples he often had to explain his parables to them because their spiritual understanding had not been developed (Mt 13:36). On one occasion when his disciples had come from buying food they encouraged him to eat something, but he told them that he had food to eat that they didn't know about. Their reaction was to ask if anyone had given him food, but he replied that it was doing the will of his Father that sustained him. Like Nicodemus, they were thinking naturally, but Jesus was talking spiritually (Jn 4:31-34).

When Jesus told the disciples that he was going to prepare a place for them so they could be with him, Thomas asked him where it was and how they could get there (Jn

14:1-5). Philip continued this natural reasoning when he asked Jesus to show them the Father. (Jn 14:6-10).

On another occasion Peter reacted with his natural understanding when Jesus told the disciples that he must go to Jerusalem and be killed. We then see Jesus' reaction to Peter's natural thinking when he said 'Get behind me Satan', adding that Peter was not thinking spiritually in God's way, but naturally, in man's way (Mt 16:21-23). Human wisdom is in opposition to God.

Until our spiritual understanding is developed, there will always be a tendency to revert to natural understanding because it is more familiar to us; but just as it would be inappropriate to revert to my native language in a foreign country simply because I had not adequately developed the language of that country, so it is totally inappropriate to revert to our natural understanding in the kingdom of God. Being spiritually blind we make natural decisions (as Eli did) and choices which are contrary to the ways of the kingdom of God. (Gal 5:16-17)

The disciples continued to develop their spiritual sight, unlike most of the scribes and Pharisees who, being unable to see spiritually, substituted natural understanding and developed their own traditions.

Sadly this is often the same today, with some religious leaders placing a natural interpretation on passages of scripture rather than seeking God for the spiritual truth that it holds. Then, like the Pharisees of old they teach from their natural understanding and turn it into church doctrine, making the scripture ineffective and producing a pseudo church - a worldly version of a spiritual church.

Jesus spoke with some believing Jews who saw themselves as the natural descendants of Abraham, and thought God was their Father. Jesus had to explain to them that although they were natural children of Abraham it did not make them spiritual children, for their heart was not right.

He told them that if they were truly Abraham's children they would do the same works as Abraham who was obedient to what God told him to do. Instead, these Jews sought to kill Jesus whom God had sent for their deliverance, showing that their father was not God but the devil (Joh 8:31-44) who only comes to steal, kill and destroy. (Jn 10:10)

Jesus repeatedly called them 'blind Pharisees'. They could not see and hear spiritually because they could not understand with their heart (Mt 13:14-15) so he told them that they must first cleanse their hearts (Mt 23:16-26).

They could only see with natural eyes and could only comprehend natural defilement so were concerned with the washing of hands and other such ordinances that can never cleanse the heart of man. (Mk 7:1-2)

Jesus had to explain that it is not the natural which defiles a man, for food goes into the mouth and exits as waste. He said it is the spiritual, or what comes out of the heart that defiles (Mt 15:10-20). We should be concerned with the cleanliness or purity of our spirit.

We have already seen how the Pharisees and Sadducees came to Jesus looking for a sign, and how Jesus told them that they could interpret natural signs like the weather, but not spiritual signs (Mt 16:1-4). They had natural sight but no spiritual discernment. They concerned themselves with the external natural appearance not the transformation of the spirit. They wore their fine clothes and liked to be called 'rabbi', but without a heart transformation this only produced a pseudo church, it was all window dressing.

God looks on the heart of man - his spirit; not the outward appearance as Samuel discovered when he was sent to anoint one of Jesse's sons to be the next king of his people. (1Sam 16:6-7)

As we have seen, it was not long before this that the people rejected spiritual leadership in favour of natural leadership when they rejected God and wanted a king like the surrounding nations (1Sam 8:4-7). They wanted natural earthly government rather than spiritual heavenly government, even though Samuel pointed out to them what it would be like (1Sam 8:10-22), telling them that this king would not give like God, but he would take and take and take – this sounds like the enemy again who only comes to steal, kill and destroy.

The Israelites were just as stubborn when God sent them prophets to give them spiritual correction; they didn't want to listen to them either. As Amos suggests, we cannot walk with God if we are not in agreement with him (Amos 3:3), and if we cannot hear his voice what hope do we have?

HUMAN WISDOM IS IN OPPOSITION TO GOD

If we do not have the spiritual eyes and ears to see the kingdom of God and hear and understand his ways it is complete folly to substitute our ways for his.

I once heard a minister quoted as saying that if the Holy Spirit left the church, most of what was going on would continue because it was ordained of man and not of God.

Natural wisdom can never replace God's wisdom, it is not even second best; it is actually in opposition to God, for it is born of the flesh and is contrary to spiritual wisdom (Gal 5:17).

As in Eli's day, the lamp of God goes out when God's ways are replaced by secular wisdom. This was the error of the five foolish virgins (Mt 25:1-13). It was the error of Judah in the days of king Josiah when they had lost the book of the law and were living by what was right in their own sight (2Kin 22). The scribes and Pharisees had the book of the law but still made the same mistake. The Israelites made the same mistake in the days of Samuel when they wanted to replace God's spiritual wisdom with the natural wisdom of a king (1Sam 8:4-7), and it is the error of many in the church today who will find themselves excluded from the kingdom of God because they have not followed the leading of the

Holy Spirit (which is the oil in the lamp of the virgins and in the temple) to become the sons of God (Jn 16:13; Rom 8:14).

Today almost every government on Earth is led by people who neither understand God's ways nor his thoughts, but they make laws based on what seems right to them. Is it any surprise that the world is in the mess that we find it? We need the government of God for as we have already seen, man is incapable of directing his own way (Jer 10:23). We need to pray for our governments.

Didn't Jesus teach us to pray that the Father's will should be done and his kingdom come to earth just as it is in heaven? (Mt 6:10)

God's wisdom and man's wisdom do not mix, just as oil and water do not mix.

Paul wrote to the Corinthian Christians telling them not to be joined together with unbelievers by doing the same unrighteous things (Eph 5:1-8), but to be separate from them if they wanted to be the sons and daughters of God (2Cor 6:14-18).

Samuel had warned the Israelites not to become like the nations round about by demanding a king, but they wouldn't listen to him (1Sam 8:1-7; Deu 18:9), they had decided what they wanted.

In the days of Ezra the Israelites joined themselves in marriage to the godless nations round about them but mercifully were brought to repentance when they listened to Ezra and separated themselves again (Ezra 10:1-17).

In the days of Nehemiah the Israelites mixed with the nations round about them and became corrupted in their ways (Neh 13:1-22) and again intermarried but were brought to repentance when they listened to Nehemiah. (Neh 13:23-31)

Mixture dilutes and weakens and can never be pure. The church is called to separate itself from what is of this world, not be joined to it (1Jn 2:15-17). Do not attempt to join the flesh to the spirit – it is unacceptable to God.

Multitudes of Christians have succumbed to the flesh in these ways today without understanding the spiritual consequences. They have joined themselves to this godless world through 'Christianized' pagan or worldly celebrations such as Christmas, Easter and Halloween by indulging their flesh just like those in the world who do not share their faith.

Keep it pure. Remember the sacrifice of the Lamb of God at Passover as the scriptures tell us, but do not run to the excess of this world that loves these celebrations.

We need to heed these words of Paul concerning separation form worldly ways, and the exhortation of Peter to abstain from the fleshly lusts of the world. (1Pet 4:1-5)

If you want the kingdom of God you will have to let go of the lusts of the flesh, you cannot serve the spirit and the flesh (Mt 7:24). God is offering you an exchange - a new life in the spirit for your old life in the flesh; you cannot have both! The kingdom of God is not a bolt-on-extra to your worldly life.

Jesus made this clear in two short parables, *The Treasure* and *The Pearl of great price* (Mt 13:44-46). You must exchange **all** that you have to obtain the prize.

This reminds me of a story I once heard of how to catch a monkey. The story says that if you fill a jar having a fairly narrow neck with nuts and secure it in some way, then a monkey will put his hand into the jar to obtain the nuts but will be unable to withdraw it with a clenched fist full of nuts. He will not let go, and remains stuck there until the hunters find him. The only way the monkey can regain his freedom is to let go of everything that is in his hand, but most will not. It is only his covetousness that deprives him of freedom and keeps him a prisoner. This is why Satan offers this world so much, it keeps them in bondage. We brought nothing into this world and we can take nothing out (1Tim 6:7), so learn to let go.

The Israelites wanted the Promised Land but they couldn't let go of their fleshly desires for Egypt (Num 11:4-6; Act 7:39). That generation never entered their Promised Land, but perished in the wilderness.

As Jesus told in the parable of *The* Sower, Many Christians today are addicted to the lusts and pleasures of this world and will bring no fruit to perfection in their lives (Mk 4:18-19; Lu 8:14) their end is to be burned (Mt 3:10; Jn 15:1-8). They are like the first generation of Israelites to come out of Egypt, they will never enter their Promised Land, the kingdom of heaven.

You cannot join the wisdom of this world to the wisdom of God, nor can you put new cloth on to an old garment, or put new wine into old wine skins (Mt 9:16-17).

WE MUST HAVE GOD'S WAYS AND THOUGHTS – OURS ARE FOLLY

We have already seen how God spoke through Isaiah telling his people that their thoughts were not his thoughts, and calling them to exchange their ways for his ways (Isa 55:7-8), and how Jeremiah declared that man was incapable of making the right decisions by himself (Jer 10:23).

Back in the time of Eli, when he was not doing his job properly, he was getting no guidance from heaven and the Israelites were being defeated by the Philistines. The people did what was right in their own sight and took the Ark of the Covenant into battle with them, expecting it to give them victory, but they were still defeated and the Ark was captured (1Sam 4:3-11). They did not have the mind of God.

We see how king Saul was told to wait for Samuel to sacrifice before the battle with the Philistines, but when Samuel was late he took it upon himself to make the sacrifice (1Sa 13:8-14) He did what seemed right to him and lost the kingdom.

The Ark of the Covenant was only to be handled by the priests (Deu 10:8), others handling holy things would die (Num 4:15), but when David had the Ark moved Uzzah did what seemed right to him by using his hand to stabilize it and died. (2Sam 6:6-7)

In the days of Josiah the king, the house of the Lord had fallen into disrepair and was being refurbished when they came across the book of the law. When the book was read, it became clear that the nation had not been walking in God's ways and following his instructions for some time, they had been doing what was right in their own sight. God was angered by their past disobedience and said he would bring evil upon them. (2Ki 22)

It is absolute folly to substitute man's wisdom, no matter how well intentioned, for God's instructions. Jesus contrasted the Spirit which brings life, with the flesh which he said is good for nothing, adding that **his** words were spirit and therefore life. (Jn 6:63)

It is the Spirit of Truth that is needed in the church today, not man's precepts. One of the most important functions of the Holy Spirit is to give the church **God's** vision to follow.

When the early church appointed deacons to help with the work, they were told to choose men who were full of the Holy Spirit, so that they could do their work with God's wisdom. (Ac 6:3)

When the Israelites followed God's instructions they had victory against their enemies.

Jericho was defeated as a result of following God's specific instructions. (Jos 6:1-5)

David followed God's specific instructions to defeat the Philistines. (2Sam 5:22-25)

If God is giving instructions and we don't follow them because we can't hear them then all our efforts are wasted, for unless God is the builder our work is in vain. (Ps 127:1)

This life could be compared to a play that must be enacted. Father is the playwright, he has written the script, Jesus is the producer and the Holy Spirit the director. We are just the actors who are called to follow the script. If we ad lib or change the script as Moses did when he struck the rock the second time instead of speaking to it (Num 20:7-12) then we are not performing God's play but our own; they are our thoughts, not his thoughts. We must remember that Father, Son and Holy Spirit are in charge at all times, even if we are the players and have been given dominion of this earth.

When God called Moses to build the tabernacle, he instructed him to make it according to the pattern that **he** had decreed (Ex 25:9). God emphasized the importance of this when he added that Moses should make sure his work was in accordance with the pattern shown him in the mount. (Ex 25:40)

When building God's temple, Solomon was admonished to build it in accordance with the pattern given to his father David by the Holy Spirit (1Chr 28:11-12), adding that the Lord had given him to understand the pattern in writing by his hand upon him. (vv19-20)

When both of these had been built in accordance with God's instructions, then His glory filled them. (Ex 40:34; 2Chr 7:1-2)

God also provided the pattern for Ezekiel's temple, and instructed him to show it to the house of Israel. (Eze 43:10)

These temples are the places where God said he would appear and meet with man (Ex 25:22; 2Chr 7:16), yet they were only a shadow of things to come. These Old Testament buildings were only natural temples made with hands, pointing the way to the spiritual temple.

How important it is to accurately portray God's instructions so that we paint the picture he wants on his canvas.

As we have already seen, Jesus always painted his Father's picture. Can you not still hear Jesus' words echoing down through the ages when he said he had not spoken of himself, but only what the Father gave him to say, because his word is life everlasting? (Jn 12:49-50) And when he said the Son can do nothing of himself, but only what he sees the Father doing? (Jn 5:19)

Oh how vital it is to have spiritual eyes and ears so that we can build and live in accordance with God's ways and thoughts.

Even when God's Old Covenant people rejected his ways, he still reached out to them to bring correction because of his love for them that they should not be lost. God does not act any differently with the church.

We see Jesus dictating letters to the seven churches of Asia. Five of them were called to repent or face serious consequences because they were not following the leading of God's Spirit. (Rev 2-3)

We have already seen how the church at Sardis had gained a name for itself as being a church that was alive, but Jesus saw it as dead (Rev 3:1). How many churches would fit that category today?

The church of Sardis is like the fig tree in the vineyard that was bearing no fruit (Luk 13:6-9), it will be cut down. Unless we are bearing fruit we are like the Pharisees that John the Baptist spoke to, and are headed for the fire. (Mt 3:10)

The church at Laodicea considered that it was rich and in need of nothing, but Jesus saw it as wretched and miserable, poor, blind and naked (Rev 3:17). How many self-satisfied, materially prosperous churches are there today? Jesus was not present in this church!

This church was not building God's kingdom, but lacking spiritual sight it was building a worldly, materialistic kingdom based on man's wisdom. It was a pseudo church.

When any church views its purpose or existence through natural eyes instead of spiritual eyes, it is a sure sign that it has missed the mark.

The church at Ephesus which had started so well had left its first love (Rev 2:4). In the beginning, this church had listened to God and been obedient to his instructions, for obedience is the evidence of love. It had prospered in doing God's work, but then it started to do what was right in its own sight. This is so often what happens to any work of God that prospers and becomes too big. We should take this as a warning.

All these churches appeared alive and prosperous outwardly, but that's not how Jesus saw them. Because he loved them he called them to repent and change their ways. Today he is calling to the churches around the globe to repent that they might be saved – yes, saved. (Rev 2:5)

There are so many that are like these five churches of Asia that think they are secure but are far from it. Instead of God's wisdom they have man's ways. Those who have spiritual ears, let them hear what the Spirit is saying to the church today, for it is those that continue in God's ways to the end that shall be saved.

Throughout the ages, those who have brought spiritual enlightenment have been rejected and persecuted, frequently by those who claim to be spiritual. Many Old Testament prophets were rejected, abused or killed. In New Testament times the disciples of Jesus suffered persecution – Paul was a prime example of this, both before and after his conversion, first persecuting the church then being persecuted. Why should we suppose it would be any different today? Persecution of God's messengers and rejection of God's ways are still common, both from secular society and that sector of the religious community that lacks spiritual sight. (Mt 10:16-25; 2Tim 3:12)

If these churches that sprung up so freshly from Paul's missionary trips had been corrupted by a wrong understanding of what constituted a real church, and Jude had to write to the believers to contend for the true faith that was once delivered to the saints (Jude 3), then how much more do you suppose it has been corrupted by the world, the flesh and the devil 2000 years later?

I have just finished reading afresh Brother Yun's reflection on his first four years living in the west. For those who are unfamiliar with this Chinese brother, you can read his story in *The Heavenly Man*. Reading between the lines, it would appear that he was quite clearly shocked by the number of churches in the west that were spiritually asleep, and how so many Christians are lulled by pleasant words of God's love for them, when in reality he is screaming at the top of his voice for his church to wake up and repent. He said that the church in the west had so much teaching available to it and yet not much of it contained the effective cutting edge of God's word. Wake up church!

Is it any surprise that other religions such as Islam are making a bid to fill the spiritual vacuum that has been created by Christian apathy, laziness and worldliness?

This is a serious issue; we are talking about the eternal destiny of millions of Christians and others that have yet to hear the gospel who they should be reaching with the truth of God's word.

We have read how Jesus spoke strongly to the religious leaders of his day, telling them that they were not entering into the kingdom, and they were hindering others from entering (Luk 11:52). Do you suppose he will speak nice kind words to those of today's churches who are doing likewise?

Wake up church! Start seeking God's will now. Study and meditate on his word and pray until you know what you should be doing, and do it wholeheartedly. Don't just regurgitate yesterday's teachings, lulling people into a false sense of security; many of them have been corrupted! Hear what God is saying to you today.

Not all who call Jesus 'Lord' will enter the kingdom, only those who **DO** the will of his Father in heaven (Mt 7:21). If you know what God's word requires of you and you don't do it, then you are sadly deceived if you think you are saved (Jas 1:21-22; Rom 2:13).

I dare not elaborate on the implications of complying with 1Pet 2:13-14 or Rom 13:1-5 for fear that it will convict over 90% of all Christians. In every country I have visited I find Christians flouting the laws of the land, even when they are not contrary to the word of God. Do we really take the scriptures seriously, or are we just hoping 'by faith' that everything will be OK whilst ignoring the scriptural conditions for entering the kingdom of God?

THE COUNTERFEIT KINGDOM OF GOD

M any Christians are wary of a coming antichrist world order which if it was possible would deceive the very elect (Mt 24:24). Secular society will always be in opposition to God's kingdom, but there already exists a counterfeit kingdom of God.

The religious leaders of Jesus' day did not have the real kingdom of God, but a pseudo kingdom of God. It was a kingdom which appeared righteous when viewed with natural sight, yet inwardly it was little different to the world from which it was supposed to be separated – Jesus called it 'hypocrisy' (Mt 23:25-28).

As we have already seen, these religious leaders were not going into the real kingdom themselves, and were preventing others from entering (Lu 11:52).

To enter into the real kingdom we must first forsake the old kingdom.

When Jesus called his disciples, we read that they left their old life and followed him immediately (Mt 4:18-22, 9:9). The disciples gave up their life to have the kingdom of God (Mt 19:27). This was not the glamorous life of a celebrity with expensive suits, fleets of luxury cars and their own private jets, but a life of persecution, rejection and death for their faith. This is what they exchanged their lives for. Paul exchanged his position of power, influence and respect in society, counting it all dung for this same life of persecution.

Today, some have exchanged their lives for the life of the Pharisee who thrives in the prominent limelight (Mt 23:1-8; Lu 20:46). They did not forsake their old lives, but enhanced them with popularity, prestige and power as portrayed by Jesus' parable of *The wicked husbandmen* (Mt 21:33-45).

Didn't Jesus say that the servant is not greater than his master, and that if he had been abused, so would they? (Mt 10:16-25)

Didn't Paul say that those who live godly lives shall suffer persecution? (2Tim 3:10-12)

The life of a disciple in the true kingdom of God is not glamorous. If we want to be Jesus' disciples we must forsake all and follow him (Lu 14:33).

The reason that it was granted to the disciples to know the mysteries of the kingdom of heaven (Mt 13:10-11), and why Paul had such mysteries revealed to him (Eph 3:3-5), was because they had exchanged their lives in this worldly kingdom and were living and working in the kingdom of God and therefore needed to understand.

By contrast to the disciples who exchanged their lives for the kingdom, we read about a rich young man who came to Jesus asking what he must do to have eternal life, but when Jesus told him to keep the commandments he replied that he had kept them since he was a boy, and asked what else he should do. Jesus then told him that if he would be perfect, he should go and sell what he had and give it to the poor so that he would have riches in heaven, and to follow Jesus. On hearing this, the young man turned away for he had great wealth. (Mt 19:16-22).

He was being offered the same exchange as the disciples, but unlike them, because he had great wealth, he was not prepared to exchange it to obtain riches in the kingdom of

God. He would not sell all of his pearls to obtain the one pearl of great value as Jesus taught in the parable.

Today, there are some in the church who entice others to give in order to get, quoting scripture to justify their plea for money (Lu 6:38; Mal 3:10). Although this is the spiritual principle of reaping what you sow (Gal 6:7), to be effective the motive must always be to give, not to get. If the motive for our giving is to get more then we have succumbed to the temptation of greed – this is not of God.

In Paul's day there were those who taught that materialistic gain was godliness (1Tim 6:5) but Paul turned this around and asserted that great gain is not materialistic but it is godliness with contentment (v6), and added that we should be content with the basic necessities of life such as food and clothing (v8). This of course is in complete agreement with the teaching of Jesus when he said we should not store up treasure on earth, but in heaven (Mt 6:19-21), and that if we make the kingdom of God our primary objective, he will provide all of our basic necessities – food, drink and clothing (Mt 6:33).

Paul continues in his letter to Timothy by saying that we brought nothing into this world and we can take nothing out when we go (1Tim 6:7), adding that many have strayed from the faith by coveting riches (vv9-10). He then tells us what Jesus meant by seeking first the kingdom of God. It is not to prosper in the power, prestige, popularity and riches of this world which so many seek, but to develop the fruit of the Spirit in our lives so that we might lay hold on eternal life (vv11-12).

Peter writes the same thing, saying that we are given great and precious promises by which we might escape the corruption that is in the world through lust (2Pet 1:4) and that by developing the fruit of the Spirit in our lives we can make sure that we are both called **and** chosen for the kingdom of God (2Pet 1:5-11).

The truth is that we don't really give up all of our worldly gains, we just invest them in our heavenly bank account, and we do this by using these riches to help those in need. When we do this, God credits our heavenly bank account. It is an exchange, in just the same way that we exchange our national currency for that of another country to which we are travelling. What proportion of your riches you squander now on self-indulgence, and what proportion you invest for your eternal future is up to you. You can use it for the short period you are on earth and consume it upon your lusts, or you can have it for eternity in heaven.

We can either sow and reap in material wealth, or we can sow in material wealth and reap in heavenly wealth. This is the only way we can transfer our natural riches into spiritual riches so that we can take them with us.

The young man in Jesus' story was being offered an exchange, but he wanted both his worldly riches and riches in the kingdom of God. He wanted both, but had to make a choice.

When this young man walked away, Jesus told his disciples how hard it was for those with riches to enter the kingdom of God (Mat 19:23-24). They become addicted to wealth and the lifestyle it brings. It is a snare of the enemy (1Tim 6:9). Are you amongst the wealthy of this world? Is your income in the top 20% - more than about £2250/year/person?

If you want the real kingdom of God rather than a counterfeit one, you will have to give up **your** life to get it.

Abram gave up his life and family in Ur of the Chaldees to follow God. (Gen 12:1-2)

Moses gave up his life of luxury and pleasure in Egypt. (Heb 11:24-26)

Elisha gave up his life and family when Elijah called him. (1Kin 19:20)

Jesus gave up his life and family. He had to be about his Father's business. (Lu 2:49)

John the Baptist gave up his life and family and went into the wilderness to preach. (Mt 3:1-3)

Jesus' disciples all gave up their lives and families to follow him. (Mt 4:18-22)

Paul gave up his life to gain and preach the kingdom. (Php 3:8)

Those who wanted and got the kingdom of God in a powerful way had to exchange their worldly kingdom to get it. This is what Jesus told the multitudes. (Lu 14:33)

This is how they got eyes to see and ears to hear.

WHICH KINGDOM ARE YOU LIVING IN?

Nebuchadnezzar, the king of Babylon was given a dream by God so that he might know future events. He didn't understand the dream and couldn't remember it until Daniel interpreted it for him (Dan 2). This dream revealed the world kingdoms that would rise and fall in the future, but also another kingdom which would replace all these others; this other kingdom being the spiritual kingdom of God. All the worldly kingdoms which follow in the footsteps of Babylon will cease to exist as the everlasting kingdom of God grows and fills the earth (Dan 2:34-35, 44-45). Which kingdom are you living in?

Peter warns us that the world will be destroyed and tells his readers that they should seriously consider what kind of lives they are living (1 Pet 3:7-12). James says that those who are friends of the world system are enemies of God (Jas 4:4) and John adds that the love of the Father is not in those who love this world that is passing away. (1Jn 2:15-17)

After this natural life we will spend eternity either in heaven or in the lake of fire but the choice, which is ours, is made now. The wise person will tune out the old life of flesh and tune in to the life of the kingdom now whilst there is still time. There is a rapidly widening rift opening up between the kingdoms of this world and the kingdom of God as this natural world gears up in its death throes to greater and greater opposition to God's eternal word prior to its destruction.

Jesus warned that many will seek to enter into the kingdom of heaven and will not be able, and tells them to strive to enter into the kingdom of God **now** (Luk 13:24). Remember the fruit test that will determine your suitability for the kingdom of heaven (Mt 7:19-20), and remember that fruit takes time to grow.

God does not make a habit of intervening in the affairs of man, but we have seen how he does so when conditions become critical and man begins to dramatically change the way earth is developing. We saw that God intervened at the Tower of Babel. (Gen 11:1-10)

God spoke to Ezekiel advising him that he will bring judgment upon unfaithful nations, and at that time people will not be spared by the righteousness of others (Eze 14:13-14).

He speaks of four principle methods of bringing judgment – war, famine, wild animals and pestilence (v21). The King James Version emphasizes that this judgment will come when sin becomes grievous.

As we look back through scripture we can see times when this occurred. In Noah's day the wickedness of mankind was great (Gen 6:5) so God brought judgment upon the whole world (vv6-7). In Lot's day the sin of Sodom and Gomorrah was grievous (Gen 18:20-21) so God brought judgment upon it (Gen 19:12-13).

In both of these times of judgment the scriptures mention the sin as being of a sexual nature (crossing the species boundary in Noah's day and homosexuality in Lot's day). Paul puts the sexual sins at the top of the lists of those lifestyles that will prevent people from entering the kingdom of God (1Cor 6:9-10; Gal 5:19-21). Both the law and the book of Revelation describe the people that live like this as abominable (Lev 18:22; Rev 21:8).

Israel was judged when David sinned by numbering the people, and was given a choice of which one of God's judgments he would prefer (1Chr 21:8-14).

Jesus tells us that God's judgment will continue to come upon this world for grievous sin. We see he mentions three of these judgments of God and adds earthquakes to the list (Mt 24:6-7; Rev 6:3-8,12). This is just the prelude to God's wrath being poured out.

Paul encourages us not to be the recipients of God's wrath for living the same way as those who will be punished (Eph 5:1-8), again putting sexual sin at the head of the list (v3), and warns us not to be deceived by such lifestyles (v6). Why should we be surprised to find that Satan, through this world and the flesh is enticing us with such things as the scriptures call 'abominable', with the laws of the land legalizing such lifestyles and even promoting them? Do not get drawn in to Satan's web of lies and deceit.

We live in a physical body in a physical world which we experience through our five physical senses. We are taught and develop our natural understanding and yet all this will pass away. It is our spirit which is eternal and which will return to God when the body returns to dust (Ecl 12:7).

For most people their whole existence is geared to this natural world which will be destroyed. If we are to enter the spiritual kingdom of God, we must retrain our minds and start to think and act spiritually. God does not want any of us to fail (2Pet 3:9), but Jesus tells us that few will succeed (Mt 7:13-14).

Isaiah heard God and made himself available to show God's people their plight. God told him to tell his people that although they could hear naturally they had no spiritual understanding, and that although they could see naturally they couldn't perceive the spiritual picture, so they were unable to understand spiritually and convert to kingdom ways and thoughts and could not be healed from their lifestyle which was preventing them from entering God's kingdom. (Isa 6:8-10)

When we read the account of *the woman at the well* (Jn 4:1-15) we see that like Nicodemus, this Samaritan woman had the same difficulty in understanding spiritually. Jesus had first asked her for a drink of natural water, but then suggested that she should be asking him for spiritual water. Her thoughts were immediately in the natural realm and she replied that he could not get water for her as he had no means of drawing it from the well. When Jesus then told her that whoever drank of this spiritual water would never thirst again, she could only understand natural thirst, and how it would save her from coming to draw natural water.

Jesus gave the same message on the last day of the Feast of Tabernacles when he stood and cried out that if anyone was thirsty they should come to him and drink spiritual waters, adding that this would not only quench their own spiritual thirst but would also flow out of them as a river flows; this spiritual water being the Holy Spirit. (Jn 7:37-39)

We see this message again depicted by Ezekiel's vision of the river of living water (Eze 47:1-12) and the holy waters that proceed from the throne of God (Rev 22:1-2).

This is not natural water as the woman at the well had supposed, but spiritual water to quench the spiritual thirst of those who thirsted for God's ways. Jesus said that those who hungered and thirsted for righteousness would be filled (Mt 5:6). Those who seek for God's righteousness shall be filled with his Holy Spirit.

Because many people cannot equate the natural picture to the spiritual reality they try to satisfy a spiritual need with a natural solution. You can't scratch an itch in the spirit.

We see a similar occurrence when Jesus fed the five thousand (Jn 6). This miracle was to point the recipients to Jesus, the spiritual bread of life, yet the people could not understand his spiritual message and asked how they could eat his physical flesh (v52). He told them not to strive for natural food which doesn't satisfy for long before more is needed, but for spiritual food that endures to everlasting life which he, the Son of man would give them. (vv26-27)

The closest they could come to understanding bread in a spiritual way was the manna that their fathers ate in the wilderness, but Jesus reminded them that their fathers ate that manna and were dead. (v49) He told them that **he** was the bread of life, and that anyone who came to him would never be hungry, and whoever believed in him would never be thirsty (v35). Again they could not comprehend this, understanding only naturally that he was the son of Joseph (v42). When Jesus repeated this message that unless the people were to eat and drink of him spiritually they would have no life in them (vv53-58), many found it such a hard saying that they turned back from following him understanding his message only in terms of cannibalism. (vv60-66)

A lack of spiritual understanding results in either walking away from God, or substituting man's natural ways in place of God's spiritual ways.

When Jesus was hungry the devil tried to get him to think naturally, but he replied that man shall not live by natural bread alone but by every spiritual word that comes from the mouth of God (Mt 4:4).

As we have seen, when Jesus was with the woman at the well his disciples tried to get him to eat the food that they had just bought, but he said he had food to eat that that they didn't know about.

The disciples presumed that someone had already given him something to eat, but he told them that his food was to do the will of him that sent him, and to finish his work. (Jn 4:31-34)

The food that Jesus was talking of was spiritual food - to be obedient to the Father's instructions.

Jesus spent over three years training his disciples and yet they still needed to have the spiritual understanding of his parables explained to them and had difficulty thinking spiritually for themselves. Although they still lacked that ability to see clearly, the disciples did not turn away or substitute the natural traditions of men as did the Pharisees, but they sought and asked until they understood. This needs to be our example.

The Pharisees taught the importance of washing hands and pots and such things which can never make anybody spiritually clean because it is all external. Jesus had criticized the Pharisees for this very reason (Mt 23:25-28), yet throughout time many in the church have extolled the virtue of cleanliness as being next to godliness. Natural cleanliness is an important social grace, but to say that it is next to godliness is pharisaical and gives a false impression. The most evil of people can be clean on the outside, but they are far from godly. Even Satan can transform himself to appear as an angel of light (2Cor 11:14-15). Natural cleanliness however is an excellent example of how we should be spiritually or inwardly, for cleanliness of spirit or purity of heart is certainly godly. We must take care not to interpret and replace spiritual truths with natural understanding.

The natural man is concerned with the natural appearance; he makes himself look smart and presentable on the outside, like the Pharisees. Now there is nothing wrong with looking smart, but God is concerned with the inner man not the outward appearance. We saw this when Samuel was sent to anoint one of Jesse's sons to be the next king of Israel (1Sam 16:6-7). God is looking for a man who is clean and presentable on the inside. Our focus must be on converting the inner man, not the outer man which perishes.

Jesus tried to get the people to understand this when he asked them what it was about John the Baptist that they went to see. Did they go to see a man dressed in soft clothes? No, because such men live in kings' houses; John was not a natural king but a spiritual prophet. He told them that they went to see a prophet although John was more than a prophet (Mt 11:8-9). John's clothing was made of camel's hair. He wore a leather apron to cover his loins; and he lived on a diet of locusts and wild honey (Mt 3:4), hardly the picture of a king.

The natural man looks on the natural appearance, but a man who seeks God must look at the spiritual appearance. The natural man is attracted to one who appears outwardly prosperous like those in kings' houses, or perhaps today it might be like those dressed in a $1000 Italian suit, being chauffeured in a fleet of luxury cars and flown in their own private jet aircraft like celebrities or royalty; whereas the spiritual man is attracted to an inward or spiritual prosperity. We have already seen that this is not the pattern of a man of God. There was nothing that would have attracted the natural man to John, or to Jesus.

Isaiah prophesied of Jesus when he said: He has no beauty or majestic appearance that we should be attracted to him when we see him (Isa 53:2). The clothing of the man of God is spiritual (Isa 59:16). We are called to be clothed inwardly with the armour of light, which is the Lord Jesus Christ (Rom 13:12-14); in other words, for our characteristics to be like his in every way.

The outward appearance does not make a man godly, for there are many wolves dressed in sheep's clothing; so don't make the same mistake as Samuel when he looked at Eliab. (1Sam 16:6-7)

Don't look with natural eyes but with spiritual eyes, otherwise you will miss the kingdom of God.

You will choose Eliab to be king instead of David.

You will by-pass John the Baptist for the smart looking Pharisee.

If you looked at Jesus with natural eyes as did the Jews, you would see the son of Joseph, for they said 'isn't this the carpenter's son?' (Mt 13:55), but if you looked with spiritual eyes as Simon Peter did, you would see the Son of God. (Mt 16:16-17)

If you looked at Jesus' mother, brothers and sisters you would see his natural family, but if you want to see his spiritual family in the kingdom of God, you must look with spiritual eyes to see those who do the will of his Father. (Mt 12:47-50)

If you looked with natural eyes as did Elisha's servant in Dothan you would see the Syrian host and defeat would stare you in the face, but if you looked with spiritual eyes as did Elisha you would see horses and chariots of fire protecting you, and assured victory. (2Ki 6:15-17)

When the word of God expresses a spiritual truth be careful not to create a doctrine based on natural understanding, but seek God for spiritual understanding, otherwise you will see the wrong picture as Eli did with Hannah, thinking she was drunk when she was in fact communing with God (1Sam 1:9-14). Your natural senses and thoughts do not reveal the kingdom of God.

FAITH OR PRESUMPTION – A REALITY CHECK

We have seen how God gave his people the conditions for blessing (Deu 28:1-2) and cursing (Deu 28:15).

We have also seen how in the time of Eli the priest the Israelites were fighting against the Philistines and were losing the battle (1Sam 4:1-11), yet amongst God's blessings Israel had the promise of victory against their enemies (Deu 28:7). The Israelites had decided to bring the Ark of the Covenant into the battle so that they would be victorious, but they were still roundly defeated and the Ark was captured. Why?

Their faith for victory was not faith as they had supposed, but presumption, for it was not founded fully on the word of God. They had expected the promise of blessing but they had met the condition for cursing. This is so true today for many in the church who are taught to claim the promise of God that they want 'by faith' without meeting God's conditions for that promise. God's promises of blessing, including victory, were for the obedient; those who obeyed his commandments and lived according to his laws. At that time the Israelites were not living in obedience to God. Eli was not even correcting his own sons; and for this failure God removed him altogether (1Sam 2:30, 34-35; 3:12-14).

Amongst the curses that follow disobedience we find defeat by enemies (Deu 28:25). God's promise was fulfilled, but not the one that those Israelites were expecting. They trusted in the Ark of God for their deliverance but were not delivered because of their failure to comply with God's conditions of deliverance. Today there are many who are similarly trusting in the name of Jesus, the Son of God for their salvation but similarly have failed to comply with God's conditions for salvation. Do you suppose God will be more lenient with these who stand by faith than he was with those Israelites? Paul tells us that if God did not spare the Israelites who were disobedient, we should take care that we who stand by faith are not similarly cut out of his kingdom. (Rom 11:17-22)

Many Christians think the curse no longer applies to them as Christ has redeemed us from the curse of the law (Gal 3:13), but the *us* that this scripture refers to is those who are in faith or truly 'in Christ', those who obey him and who have been transformed (Rom 12:2) to become new creatures (2Cor 5:17), it is not for the disobedient who Paul tells us will still receive the judgment of God (Rom 13:1-2; Heb 10:26-29), for disobedience is the manifestation of unbelief or lack of faith (Rom 11:17-22) as was the case of the Israelites under Moses (Heb 4:1-2, 11), and is the manifestation of a lack of love (Jn 14:24). We have already seen from the parables of Jesus that those who listen to his instructions but do not obey them will be excluded from the kingdom of heaven.

Peter confirms that judgment will begin with God's people, and only the truly righteous shall be saved (1Pet 4:17-18). John also emphasizes that those who do not manifest works of righteousness are not born of God but are children of the devil (1Jn 3:10). It is only those who have purified their souls by obedience to God which results in works of righteousness that are born again (1Pet 2:22-23).

Some preachers find these scriptures do not fit into their understanding of the doctrine of salvation by grace and try to separate the judgment of believers and their works. Don't be deceived the curse is still upon disobedient Christians (Eph 5:6-8).

The Israelites under Moses' leadership perished without ever entering their Promised Land because they did not obey God (Josh 5:6), even though God was with Moses and had made the Promised Land available to them.

In the time of Joshua God made a promise to him that he would be with him just as he had been with Moses (Josh 1:3-5). Joshua was told to go and possess the land that God had promised, and God promised that nobody would be able to stand up to him in battle. This of course is the blessing for obedience (Deu 28:7).

God gave them victory at Jericho, but he had given them an instruction which they were to obey; they were to keep themselves from the *accursed thing*, and gather the silver and gold for the Lord's treasury (Josh 6:18-19). One man disobeyed and took some silver, some gold and an accursed thing - a Babalonish garment (Josh 7:21). Babylon is always associated with rebellion against God even though God used Nebuchadnezzar to fulfil his promises (Jer 25:8-9). The result of this man's disobedience was to move the Israelites out of blessing and into cursing.

In their very next battle against the little city of Ai they were roundly defeated by their enemies. When Joshua asked God why this had happened, God told him that they **could not** stand against their enemies because of this sin and said that he would not be with them any more until they had cleansed themselves and destroyed the perpetrator. (Josh 7:11-13)

If the Israelites wanted to inherit the blessings of God they had to be ruthless about sin and so do we, for all disobedience to God is sin. After defeating Jericho, the Israelites expected to defeat Ai with ease, but their expectation was presumptuous. They had trusted in the promises of blessings which were given to Joshua, but had failed to comply with God's conditions for that blessing of victory and so were defeated. Today there are many who are similarly trusting in the promises of God which are given to them in scripture (2Cor 1:20), but have failed to comply with God's conditions for those promises. Do you suppose God will be more lenient with these?

The Israelites had treated the Ark of the Covenant as nothing more than a talisman; thinking it would bring them victory, but victory was not through faith in the Ark, it was through faith in (obedience to) the God of the Ark. Today so many Christians make the same mistake, thinking the name of Jesus will assure them of all the promises of God, but as we have already noted, it is the closeness of our relationship to God by becoming like Jesus or being truly 'in Christ' that makes the promises of God available to us (2Cor 1:20), for to be *in Christ* implies obedience to his words. (Jn 14:20-24)

God has given us great and precious promises but sin negates those promises as Joshua found out. Make no mistake; the promises of God are **CONDITIONAL**; not on his part, but on our ability to access them. In the Hebrew text all of God's promises are in the perfect tense; as far as God is concerned they are a 'done deal'. Multitudes of Christians today think of God's promises as their automatic **right**, just like the Israelites when they attacked Ai, but they are sorely mistaken. Both Old and New Testaments are full of God's promises which some like to name and **claim** for themselves, but so often they don't comply with the conditions by which they can access them and then, like Joshua, wonder why they haven't received the promise they expected.

It is like having a complimentary ticket to an event and finding that you are refused entry because there are conditions printed on the ticket which you have failed to meet. For temporal things like a free ticket to an event this brings disappointment and discouragement, but for eternal issues such as your salvation it is nothing short of a total catastrophe.

GOD SAYS – COME UP HIGHER

How many times have you heard the Lord speak through prophecy calling his church to come up higher? What does this mean and how can we achieve it?

As we have already seen, the kingdom of God and the kingdoms of this world are two different realms which do not mix, but co-exist in the same time and place. The kingdom of God is of an infinitely higher order than the natural kingdoms of this earth.

Jesus came *down* to earth from heaven for our benefit. The devil also came *down* to earth from heaven. (Rev 12:12) The direction *down* implies moving from the higher realm to the lower, and *up* would be the reverse (Jn 3:13). So when God calls his church to come up higher he wants us to move into a greater realm of authority by our ways becoming more closely aligned to his.

Let us look at some examples of people that chose to trade a superior status for an inferior one by moving downwards.

Satan had an exalted position in heaven and traded it for the kingdoms of this world which he later offered to Jesus in an attempt to keep him down also (Luk 4:5-7). Apart from Jesus and Satan we see that some of the angelic realm came down (Jude 6). Some angels were tempted by the flesh just like Adam and Eve, but this time it was human flesh that brought them down (Gen 6:2-4). One third of the angels followed Satan in this downward move. (Rev 12:4, 9)

Adam lived in the Garden of Eden, a type of paradise on earth, but together with Eve he chose to follow his natural senses and disobey God and ended up exchanging his superior living for a vastly inferior one where he had to toil for his existence when he was cast out of the garden. (Gen 3:17-24)

Esau had an inheritance as the firstborn, but exchanged it for a bowl of stew. (Gen 25:29-33)

Judas had a part in establishing the kingdom of God on Earth, but exchanged it for thirty pieces of silver (Mt 26:15). Jesus said it would have been better for him if he had never been born. (Mk 14:21)

In his parable of *The Good Samaritan* (Luk 10:30) Jesus told the story of a man who went down from Jerusalem to Jericho, from a higher to a lower realm both spiritually and physically. As a result he was robbed and left for dead - this is what Satan does (Jn 10:10). After the Samaritan, who is a picture of Jesus, cared for and restored him, he was left with a choice – to continue down to Jericho or to go back up to Jerusalem.

In his parable of *The Prodigal Son* (Luk 15:11) we see the father's house as a picture of the superior or spiritual status of life in the kingdom of God, but one son decided to leave this behind and indulge in a worldly lifestyle which appealed to his flesh, resulting in his destitution until he came to his senses and realized that he had made a bad move, which he reversed by going back up to his father's house.

Satan is always tempting us with the desires and pleasures of the flesh. These stories all remind me of some of the early traders who travelled to the Americas. They offered to exchange pretty, colourful but worthless beads for pieces of native gold bearing rock that had no physical attraction.

Similar stories in scripture go on and on, with Mephibosheth living in Lodebar, a place of no bread, until David brought him up to his table and restored his inheritance to him (2Sam 9:9-10).

Abraham, Isaac and Jacob all went down from the land God had promised them, resulting in trouble. Jacob's descendants found themselves in bondage for 400 years in Egypt (Gen 15:13), a picture of this world, until God sent Moses to deliver them and bring them back up into the Promised Land (Ex 3:8). Even then they would not follow Moses willingly, and in their hearts turned back again into Egypt (Act 7:37-39), remembering the fish, cucumbers, melons, leeks, onions and garlic (Num 11:4-6) which all appealed to their fleshly senses. When they eventually came into the Promised Land, they rejected God's higher authority and wanted a worldly king like the nations round about. (1Sam 8:4-7)

Nimrod also rejected God's higher authority and rebelled by building Babylon and staying in the plain of Shinar. (Gen 9:1, 11:1-4) Babylon represents the kingdoms of this world which are to be destroyed (Dan 2:31-45), and even though Babylon was destroyed as a world power, God is still calling his people to come out of spiritual Babylon (Rev 18:1-4) if they want to be his sons and daughters (2Cor 6:14-18).

We do see a spark of light from Ruth, a Moabitess whose father-in-law and his two sons went down into Moab from Israel and died, but she reversed the direction and went back up to Israel with her mother-in-law Naomi and married Boaz to become the great grandmother of king David (Ruth 1:1,16,22; 4:9-10).

All of these scriptures show us examples of how we are enticed by the natural world, but God is calling us up into our spiritual inheritance.

We must be like Jesus and not only resist these temptations but strive to reverse the direction and press into the kingdom of God. We must be like the salmon at spawning time and swim upstream against the flow of this world.

Some years ago God gave me a picture to illustrate the need to rise up. He showed me a scene at the seaside. The beach was backed by a cliff as high as the White Cliffs of Dover and was packed with families; some sitting at the foot of the cliff, some playing on the foreshore, others paddling in the shallows and yet others swimming. The sea represented this world, and the cliff top, the kingdom of God. God was calling people to come up higher, but the sun was shining and they were having too much of a good time to listen to God. I noticed the currents pulling the swimmers out to sea and watched them drown. Those paddling in the shallows didn't notice that the tide was coming in, and soon found themselves in deeper water. When the tide turned they were sucked out to sea and were lost. Others sitting above the high water line thought they were safe until a tsunami came in and swept them all away. Virtually nobody had heeded the call of God to come up to the top of the cliff.

The pull of this world is like the lure of Egypt was for those Israelites that had been delivered, always trying to draw us away from God and back to Egypt to destroy us.

The moral of this picture is not to get entangled with this world even casually, and not even to hang around on the periphery (2Cor 6:14-18; Rev 12:15).

It is important to resist temptation and not be seduced by worldly treasure (Mt 6:19-21) as depicted by Vanity Fair in John Bunyan's *The Pilgrim's Progress* even if it does appear pleasing to the eye. For what advantage is it if we should gain the whole world (as Satan offered Jesus) and lose our soul (Mt 16:26)?

What will you trade **your** soul for? A bowl of stew? Thirty pieces of silver?

Can't you hear the voice of God calling you out of Babylon and up into his kingdom (Rev 18:4)?

During a time of praise I saw the kingdom of God depicted as a city with what appeared to be some kind of transparent dome over it. There were many Christians standing outside peering in with interest but not entering. They were just like those Israelites who would not go up into the Promised Land when they were told to do so; they were in unbelief and therefore disobedient.

Moses delivered the Israelites from Egypt but that was only the first half of his remit; he was then to bring them up **into** the Promised Land (Ex 3:8) but that generation rebelled and never entered. Unlike Moses, they never even saw the land from the outside (Deu 34:1-6).

Jude reminds us that after saving the Israelites from Egypt, God later destroyed them because they would not enter into the Promised Land (Jude 5). We read that they could not enter in because of unbelief (Heb 3:19). When the spies were too afraid to go up into the land it was the final straw; they had seen God's miracles but would not obey and instead wanted to return to Egypt (Num 14:1-4, 11, 22-23).

The people were afraid. They didn't think they could conquer the land, but God never asks us to do what we can't do. We do what we can, and he does what we can't. Jericho was one of the high walled cities the Israelites didn't believe they could conquer, but they didn't have to knock the walls down, God knocked them down when they obeyed him.

The Israelites did not believe so they did not obey, and they did not enter in. The list of those who will not enter the kingdom of God but burn in the fire is headed by the fearful and unbelieving (Rev 21:8).

Thomas said he didn't know the way into the kingdom (Jn 14:1-5). Do you know the way? Does your church know?

We must hear God's voice as Peter did when he was in prison, we must listen and obey his instructions; it is the difference between eternal life and death. It is the difference between the wise and foolish virgins (Mt7:24-27). If Peter had not heard and obeyed he would have perished in prison just as the Israelites perished in the wilderness, and like many Christians will perish in their wilderness without ever entering the kingdom of God.

So how do we come up higher?

Who shall ascend? – He that has clean hands and a pure heart (Psa 24:3). Don't read this scripture and say 'I have clean hands and a pure heart – by faith'. Either you have or you haven't, don't deceive yourself. If you have to add the suffix *by faith*, then it is unlikely that you have clean hands and a pure heart and need to repent; there's no reality in your life. If you have real faith **you** will cleanse your hands and purify your hearts. (Jas 4:8)

Who shall abide? – He that is righteous (Psa 15:2). Don't say 'I have the righteousness of Christ – by faith'. Either God sees you as righteous or he doesn't. Those who are declared righteous are those who do acts of righteousness; those who do not are children of the devil. This is the distinction between a son of God and a child of the devil (1Jn 3:7-10). Jesus made this very plain when speaking with some *believing* Jews who wanted to kill him. They were not doing the same works of obedience that their father Abraham had done and to whom God imputed righteousness. (Jn 8:31-44)

The way of the just (righteous) is upright (Isa 26:7). The way into the kingdom is the way of holiness (Isa 35:8). This is the way you are being shown, so make sure you walk in it (Isa 30:21). Don't experience the wrath of God, walk as children of light. (Eph 5:6-8)

THE TEMPLE OF GOD

We have seen how Moses' tabernacle and Solomon's temple were God's design. At the very heart of Moses' tabernacle in the Ark in the holiest place were God's commandments. It was only after they had been put into place that God's glory filled this tabernacle and the shell came to life (Exo 40). We see how Solomon's temple came to life also after the ark containing the commandments was brought up into its place. (2Chr 5)

This is no different from the shell of man who became a living soul when the breath of God entered into him, or Ezekiel's army of dry bones which came to life when the breath if God entered them. (Eze 37)

If God is to live in the temple then his instructions must be the basis of all that goes on. God told Solomon that if he did not keep his statutes and commandments then he would abandon the temple he had built. (2Chr 7:19-21)

God makes it clear throughout scripture that when his people turn away from his commandments judgment follows; this was part of his covenant with them (De 28:58-63), but he also said that when he brings judgment upon the land in the form of famine (lack of rain), locusts or pestilence (Ez 14:13-21, Joel 1:4) then if his people will turn back to him he will restore all things. (2Ch 7:13-14, Joel 2:25)

It is God's desire and intention to restore his creation, including mankind, to its former glory.

Some will say that these judgments are Old Testament law and that Christians are no longer under the law or its curse, (Deu 28:15, Gal 3) but we have already seen how disobedient Christians are still subject to the curse, which is in evidence by the multitudes of Christians who ask why they are still experiencing these curses. Didn't Jesus say that even the smallest part of the law would not pass away whilst heaven and earth existed (Mt 5:18)? Those who do not walk in God's ways are still subject to the penalties of disobedience, (Eph 5:1-7, Heb 10:26-29) which Paul equates to unbelief. (Rom 11:17-23)

The law is to the Old Testament what faith is to the New Testament, but God's standards do not change (Psa 119:89; Mal 3:6). Living by faith does not negate compliance with the law, but it fulfils the law by exceeding its requirements. Jesus did not come to destroy the law but to fulfil it. (Mt 5:17)

Jesus said that the two greatest commandments are to love God with all your being and to love your neighbour as yourself, adding that the whole of the law is dependent on these two commandments (Mt 22:37-40). He then told one of the scribes that agreed with this that he was not far from the kingdom of God (Mk 12:28-34). Paul concurs with this when he says that whoever loves others has fulfilled the law (Ro 13:8-9), adding that love will do nothing evil, so if we love our neighbour in deed we automatically fulfil the law.

A set of commandments written on tablets of stone cannot save us, it is the changed heart that results from understanding and being converted to God's ways that conforms us to the image of God's Son, Jesus, (Rom 8:29) and hence makes us fit for the kingdom of heaven.

Once our hearts are fully converted we no longer need the law, for the law is to show transgressors their sin. Whoever is born of God does not sin (1Jn 3:8-9; 1Jn 5:18).

The desire of our hearts will then be to do God's will because we have become conformed to his ways; we will not want to oppose God in any way. (Gal 3:24-25)

When we have been truly recreated in the image of Jesus then we will have become a new creature (2Cor 5:17) from the inside out.

It is also correctly said that those who are truly in Christ are saved by grace (Eph 2:8-9), yet grace clearly existed under the Old Covenant for it is not God's will that any should perish, but that all should come to repentance (2Pet 3:9). This scripture is a quote from the Old Testament where God says that if the wicked stop doing what is wrong and do what is right they will not die, but warns that they must continue to live righteously (Eze 33:11-16) as Jesus taught also when he told those who were healed or forgiven not to sin any more (Jn 5:14, 8:11) adding elsewhere that those who continue to the end shall be saved (Mt 24:13), for if we return to our sin like the pig to its wallowing in the mire (2Pet 2:20-22), then the evil spirit will return with others. (Lu 11:24-26)

Sin is sin, no matter when it is committed, whether under the Old or New Covenant. The penalty is still the same, and the conditions for release from that penalty are still the same – repentance. This is grace, it is not earned or deserved; it is God's gift freely given, but we are unable to receive and keep it without repentance and righteous living. God's mercy and forgiveness will be experienced by all who truly turn away from their transgressions and obey his commandments, for without obedience we cannot be in Christ neither he in us. (1Jn 2:3-5)

Jesus said that it is those who keep his commands that love him, and that he will come and live in them, but those who do not keep his commands do not love him. (Jn 14:21-24)

Now the scripture tells us that God does not live in temples made with hands. (Act 7:47:48)

As we have mentioned, the Old Testament tabernacle and temples were just a shadow of things to come. Jesus' death put an end to the Temple sacrifices (Heb 9:25-28). He told his disciples to stop looking towards the temple of stone (Mt 24:1-2).

Paul declares that **we** become the temple of God, and God lives in us (1Cor 3:16). We become the living stones of the temple which is God's dwelling place (1Pet 2:5). We are no longer to go into the temple to meet with God; God comes to meet with us in our temple when our spirit is in one accord with his Spirit (Rom 8:16).

In the New Testament we see the distinction between these two temples by the use of two different Greek words; *hieron* – the temple buildings, and *naos* – the actual sanctuary.

Hieron is always used of the temple made with hands, the temple of stone; whereas the temple that is made of flesh, our bodies, is only ever expressed by the word *naos*.

Jesus said 'Destroy this temple (naos) and I will raise it up in three days' (Jn 2:19-21), but when Jesus talked about the destruction of the old temple he used the word *hieron*. (Mt 24:1-2)

The true church as a living organism made of flesh has replaced the old temple of stone and has become the dwelling place of God in the same way that God said he would replace the heart of stone with a heart of flesh. (Eze 36:26)

Paul says that we are the living temple of God, and asks what we have in common with idols, unrighteousness and darkness? He commands us to separate ourselves from these things and not to have contact with what is unclean if we want to be received by God and to be his sons and daughters. (2Cor 6:14-18)

We have seen that these man made temples were only a shadow of things to come; yet if God went to so much trouble to ensure that temples made by man were fashioned in accordance with his instructions, how much more should we who are his permanent residence be fashioned in accordance with his instructions? He is the architect; we are only the builders under the direction of His Spirit. This is why Paul warns the builders to take care what and how they build. (1Cor 3:10)

At the dedication of Solomon's temple, God said that he had chosen this house that Solomon had built and sanctified it, but that if the people turned away from his commandments then he would abandon it (2Ch 7:16-22). This was fulfilled in Jesus' day, for he said to the scribes and Pharisees that their house had been abandoned by God (Mt 23:38), and in AD70 it was raised to the ground by the Roman legions.

Don't you realize that God will do the same to you if you cease to obey his commands?

Didn't Paul warn the church of this very thing? (Rom 11:17-23)

Today, many people both Christians and Jews are looking for the temple to be rebuilt, but they are looking for a temple of stone, not a temple of flesh. They are looking for a man made temple not a God made temple. They are looking for that which God has done away with, not recognizing that God's temple has been under construction since the time of Jesus, and is nearing completion. They are looking with natural eyes for a natural temple (which may well be built) rather than using spiritual eyes and seeing a spiritual temple.

They do not expect the man of sin to come until this temple is built, because he has to sit in it (2Th 2:4), however the word used for temple here is not *hieron* but *naos*. He will not be sitting in a temple of stone, but enthroned in the hearts of flesh of those Christians who do not obey God; those who have stopped short or fallen away from following the truth. Satan craves your worship and your obedience to him.

Paul writes that we become the servant of whoever we obey (Ro 6:16), and Jesus said that because people will disregard God's law their love for him would grow cold, but that those who continue in his ways **to the end** will be saved (Mt 24:12-13). Notice how this agrees with God's words to Ezekiel in the Old Testament. (Eze 33:11-15)

If you are not obeying God, then Jesus is not living in you. (Jn 14:23-24)

If Jesus is not enthroned in your temple then guess who is?

How can we tell who is truly the lord of our lives?

Jesus said that he would live in the hearts of those who keep his commandments. (Jn 14:23)

When Jesus is Lord of our lives then we will exhibit the characteristics of the King, not those of our old nature. What is born of the flesh is flesh, and what is born of the Spirit is spirit (Jn 3:6). If we still manifest the characteristics of our old nature, then Jesus is not yet fully Lord of our lives.

God's characteristics occur naturally when our heart is renewed, they are not manufactured or forced by us, even though obedience is the first step. These characteristics are grounded in love and compassion, in mercy and forgiveness; they are the fruit of the Spirit. This is the Spirit that Jesus sent to us on the Day of Pentecost so that he might abide in us. (Joh 14:15-17)

Those who have received Jesus have been given the power **to become** the sons of God (Jn 1:12), the power to be born again by being conformed to God's Spirit; (Jn 1:13) they are those who are led by the Spirit that he sent. (Rom 8:14)

Satan does not want to sit in an empty stone temple (*hieron*). He wants **you** to bow down and worship him. He wants **you** to obey him. He wants to sit in **your** temple (*naos*), **your** holy place, **your** heart, showing that he is **your** god. (2The 2:3-4)

Unless you have been truly transformed, that is exactly where he is right now.

What can we do to dethrone Satan?

James writes that if we submit ourselves to God and resist the devil, he will flee from us (Jas 4:7). Many Christians try to resist the devil but keep on yielding to his temptations. It's rather like people who set themselves New Year's resolutions but after a short while are back in their old ways. The old nature keeps rearing its head. The key is in the first part of the verse - *Submit yourselves therefore to God* – first.

To submit to God means to change your ways and thoughts for his, which requires obedience to His commands. Trying to resist the devil without first submitting to God is futile.

Isaiah writes that if the wicked man forsakes his way, and the unrighteous man his thoughts, and returns to the Lord's ways and thoughts then he will freely pardon them (Isa 55:7). This again is an example of God's grace in the Old Testament.

CLEANSE YOUR TEMPLE

Y our temple is unacceptable to God as a dwelling place until it has been thoroughly cleansed of anything which defiles.

Let us look back to the natural temple and king Hezekiah's counsel for the Levites.

Hezekiah called the Levites to sanctify themselves and to sanctify the temple of God and remove the filthiness from the holy place. He said that their fathers had sinned against God and done that which was evil in his eyes; they had forsaken him, shut the doors of the temple, turned away from his temple and turned their backs on him. They had extinguished the lamps (2Ch 29:5-8). Remember the implications of this from the passage on Eli the priest, for the lamps were never to be extinguished.

The Levites obeyed Hezekiah and restored the house of the Lord to its former glory (2Ch 29:15-19).

Jesus showed us the same example when he cleansed the temple in Jerusalem. (Jn 2:13-16)

After the temple was rebuilt in Ezra's day, we see that Nehemiah set about rebuilding the walls of the city. We read how Tobiah was first grieved to hear that the walls were going to be rebuilt (Neh 2:10), then he spoke, mocking the whole idea (Neh 2: 19). When he heard that the work had commenced he was angry and indignant and mocked the efforts of those who had started to build (Neh 4:1-3) but when he saw that the wall was progressing well he became very angry and actively fought against the work (Neh 4:7-8) purposing to kill them (Neh 4:11). He had the spirit of his father the devil.

This man Tobiah who was actively against the work of God was joined to the Jews by marriage. Both he and his son had married Jewish women, and he had many supporters in Judah (Neh 6:17-19). Instead of being separated unto the Lord, many people were joined to this evil man.

In the days of both Ezra and Nehemiah we see how the people were called to repent of wrong unions by separating themselves from their strange wives (Ne 13:1-3). Let us remind ourselves that Moses had commanded them not to inter-marry with the nations round about them (Deu 7:1-4), and that true sons and daughters of God remain separated from such liaisons (2Cor 6:14-18). Yet we see that such marriages had taken place among the people before this time with the disastrous consequences that God had warned them about. (Jgs 3:5-7; 1Kin 11:1-8)

After all that Tobiah had done, we read that Eliashib the priest who was in charge of the house of God was **allied** to Tobiah and prepared a great room for him **in the temple** where all the offerings should have been (Ne 13:4-5).

You are the priest over **your** house of God. Who or what are you joined to that has taken up residence in your temple?

We read that Nehemiah came to Jerusalem, and understood the evil that Eliashib had done in preparing a room in the courts of the house of God for Tobiah. He was sorely grieved and threw all of Tobiah's household stuff out of the room and commanded it to be cleansed and then restored to its proper function. (Ne 13:7-9)

This is **your** job, make sure you do it **now**, otherwise it will remain! If the temple of stone needed to be cleansed then how much more do we need to make sure our temple is cleansed and that God's law is in our hearts? (Psa 40:8)

Jesus did the same thing when he went into the temple and turned over the tables of the money changers, saying that they had turned a house of prayer into a den of thieves. (Mt 21:12-13)

Paul also told us to cleanse our temples when he wrote that we should put off the old man which is corrupt, be renewed in the spirit of our minds, and put on the new man which, just like God, is created in righteousness and true holiness (Eph 4:22-24). We should have nothing to do with the unfruitful works of the evil one. (Eph 5:11)

Let us pay attention to the importance of hearing God. If we can't hear God we can't be led by him. Elijah could not hear God on Mount Horeb until the inner turmoil had gone, then he heard the still small voice. (1Kin 19:11-13)

It is essential that we cleanse our temples as Hezekiah, Nehemiah and Jesus have shown us.

Who is still joined to Tobiah in some way?

Who still has a place in their temple for Tobiah?

What unholy thoughts, ways or characteristics are still hidden in **your** heart?

God is calling you to cleanse your temple to make it fit for the king. Now it's up to you.

THE BALL IS IN
OUR COURT AND
THE CLOCK IS TICKING

W hen God created the heavens and the earth he didn't rest until the seventh day when his work was finished (Gen 2:2). We have already established that Jesus finished his work and is sat down at the right hand of the Majesty on high (Heb 1:3). You will note here that Jesus is described as being in the express image of God. Like his Father, he didn't sit down until his work was finished.

Today we have vast numbers of Christians who have sat down and are awaiting their time to go to heaven but, like those Israelites of Moses' day, they have not believed in the biblical sense. They are still in unbelief because, like those Israelites they have not obeyed the commands of God, so they have not finished their work and they are not yet conformed to his image. This is why the author of Hebrews warns us to make haste to enter into God's rest, so that nobody will make the same mistake as those Israelites and fail to enter in because of their own disobedience. (Heb 4:11)

It is worth mentioning here that warnings are given throughout the book of Hebrews telling us that it is only those who continue faithfully to the end who will inherit the promises (Heb 3:6,14; 4:14; 10:23,26,35-36,39; Mt 10:22; 24:13).

Many have been taught that they are already seated together with Jesus in heavenly places. This tells us that we have been given the same authority as him, but Paul's teaching here refers to those who have truly changed and no longer walk in the ways of this world (Eph 2:1-6). As we have already seen we have the work of personal transformation which is our responsibility, and the work of the kingdom to be doing until Jesus returns. To think we can do nothing is a fatal mistake which puts us in the same shoes as the servant who was given one talent and did nothing with it (Mt 25:14-30). We deceive ourselves if we take extracts from the word of God and make them say what we want them to say. Paul spoke to the elders from the church of Ephesus telling them that he had not picked the scriptures he had taught them, but had given them the *whole of God's counsel*. (Act 10:27)

We cannot afford to waste our time on frivolous trivial pursuits as do the people of this world, when our eternal destiny is still not fully confirmed. Jesus said we should strive to enter through the narrow way that leads to eternal life, for many will try to enter in and will not be able. (Lu 13:24)

Some have never really begun their work of transformation that Paul preaches, so they have not begun to attain that heavenly realm. It is not faith but presumption to think otherwise, and presumption does not save us, it only deceives us.

William Booth, the founder of the Salvation Army was shown a vision which was published in *The War Cry* 15 June 1885 and well worth reading as it shows so much of the church to be sitting down waiting and involved in the unfruitful trivialities of this world that the gentiles seek after (Mt 6:31-34). It is reproduced on page 21 of the excellent biography entitled *William and Catherine* by Trevor Yaxley. He saw the hypocrisy of those who professed to have become

Christians, but whose lives denied their faith by their lack of godly concern. (Tit 1:16)

The ball is in our court, there is work for us to do and we would be foolish to rest from that work until we have attained our goal. Even when our work of transformation has been accomplished we have work to do in the kingdom of God.

The door to the kingdom will remain open for a limited time only. When Moses delivered the Israelites out of bondage in Egypt, just as Jesus delivered us from sin, there was a limited time set by God for the Israelites to enter their Promised Land. It was not a physical time, but was dependent upon their response to him. We read that when God called 'time' on that generation all but two of the adults were consigned to perish in the wilderness, having had the promise of a land flowing with milk and honey, but never entering it because of their disobedience. God had delivered them from Egypt because they could not do that themselves, but then the ball was in their court. All they had to do was obey God's instructions given through Moses and they would have walked into the Promised Land, less than a two week trek, but they spent their lifetime resisting God.

Although they followed Moses in the way, they murmured because of the hardness of the way – they wanted it to be easy, they just wanted to go on an excursion, but that wasn't God's plan. They needed to go through *cold turkey* (detoxification) to remove their addiction to the lusts of Egypt from their system.

Similarly God sent Jesus to set us free from sin, and now the ball is in our court, all we have to do is obey God's instructions given to us through Jesus. As Jesus has the highest authority we would be wise to listen and obey. Don't resist him as those Israelites did (Heb 3:7-11), or as the religious leaders did in Stephen's day (Act 7:51), but be led by the Spirit of God into your Promised Land and become a true son of God (Rom 8:14). Don't expect the way to be easy, it's not a Sunday afternoon excursion. God will test each of us just like he did with those Israelites, to see if we will obey him when the going gets tough.

When Jesus was shown the temple buildings by his disciples he told them that the temple would be destroyed. They asked him when this would happen and what would be the signs of his coming and of the end of the age (Mt 24:1-3). Jesus then went into great detail to give them the signs that would herald the destruction of the temple and his return. These are two separate events which are answered together, but are probably easier to distinguish from one another by studying Luke 21.

After he had given them the signs he told them that only his Father in heaven knows the day and the hour because he is all knowing (Mt 24:36). Not even Jesus knew, but many Christians think they know better, and have tried to work out a date; so far all have been wrong. The reason being that **there is no fixed date**. The Lord's return is not dependent on a specific time, but on the condition of men's hearts.

It is like the Doomsday Clock. The Doomsday Clock is a theoretical clock established in 1947 at the University of Chicago to estimate how close the world is to global disaster. As the world approaches global disaster, so the clock approaches midnight. At the time of writing, the Doomsday Clock stands at six minutes to midnight. To date, the time on the clock has been altered 19 times. When conditions between nations improve the time regresses, when conditions become more tense the time advances. Thus there is no specific time that the clock will strike twelve; it is dependent on man's relationship with God and his fellow man.

Jesus gave them a picture of the conditions on earth at the time of his return as being as it was in the days of Noah and the days of Lot (Lu 17:26-30). It was the condition of men's hearts that caused God to call judgment on the world in those days, not a specific date. (Gen 6:5)

We are told to watch and be ready (Mt 24:42, 44), and to make sure we are doing our master's will when he returns, otherwise we will be cut out like a cancer and punished in the same way as the hypocrites (Mt 24 45-51). You will remember that just before this, in Matthew 23 Jesus had repeatedly referred to the scribes and Pharisees as hypocrites, and he had said that unless our righteousness exceeds that of the scribes and Pharisees we will never enter the kingdom of heaven (Mt 5:20). Take this as a warning from God.

FAITH AND WORKS

To many Christians, *faith* and *works* are something of a conundrum. They know that we are saved by grace through faith not works but mistakenly regard all works as legalism, consigning them to the rubbish bin.

Paul taught that we are saved by grace through faith not works (Eph 2:8-9) but then James writes that without works our faith is not validated (Jas 2:17-18). Paul tells us that Abraham was justified by faith not works (Rom 4:2-3) based on one scripture (Gen 15:6) and James says that Abraham was saved by works (Jas 2:21-23) based on another scripture (Gen 22:2, 15-16).

In the same letter that Paul writes about being saved by faith not works, he also tells the church that they must stop living in their old corrupt ways, change their thinking, and start living the life of one who is truly righteous and holy, just as God is. (Eph 4:22-24) – works!

Paul writes that no flesh shall be made righteous by the deeds of the law (Rom 3:20) and the author of the book of Hebrews tells us that the Old Covenant is ready to vanish away (Heb 8:13), but Jesus says that not the smallest part of the law will be superseded until heaven and earth pass away, linking this to righteousness. (Mt 5:18-20)

When the Philippian jailor asks what he must do to be saved, Paul tells him to believe on the Lord Jesus Christ (Act

16:31), but in his letter to the church at Philippi he writes that he does not yet consider himself to be perfect and is still not assured of his own salvation and is continually pressing on towards the mark and exhorts them to do likewise. (Php 3:11-15)

It was only just before his execution after he had continued faithfully to the end of his life that he wrote to Timothy telling him that he was ready to be offered. He said he had lived his life and been faithful to God's calling, and so there would **now** be a crown of righteousness awaiting him (2Tim 4:6-8).

Didn't Jesus say that God so loved the world that he gave his only begotten Son that anyone who believes in him should not perish but have everlasting life (Jn 3:16)? He then went on to say that in the resurrection those who have done good will have life and those who have done evil will have damnation (Jn 5:29), appearing to move the goalposts from faith to works.

Whenever we take isolated scriptures rather than looking at the overall picture of scripture we are at risk of forming a doctrine that is misleading or even in error. To understand concepts like grace, faith (belief) and works we must have the whole counsel of God and not ascribe generalised meanings to them that give our flesh an excuse to continue its reign in our lives.

Real faith always produces results; it is not just an ethereal concept. If a person truly believes in Jesus then it has a life changing effect which is visible by their actions – it manifests itself in **works**.

We do not do works to save ourselves, for that is legalistic, but works of righteousness flow naturally from a transformed heart.

The religious establishment of Jesus' day had taken certain scriptures and added traditions which may even have been based on the scriptures but had produced doctrine that actually made the word of God null and void. For this reason it is vital to understand the principles of scripture and the heart of God.

The Jews of Jesus' day had a very rigid understanding of the Mosaic Law, criticising Jesus for working on the Sabbath, based on the scripture which declares that whoever works on the Sabbath shall be put to death (Ex 31:15), not truly understanding the purpose of the Sabbath which was made for man, rather than man being made for the Sabbath as Jesus corrected them (Mk 2:27). Today there are still a number of Ultra-Orthodox Jews who will violently oppose anything that they consider to be work on the Sabbath, even throwing stones at an ambulance (Mt 12:11-12).

God complained to his people through Isaiah telling them that although they were following the law by bringing offerings and making sacrifices, offering incense and celebrating the feasts, it was all unacceptable to him because their hearts remained unchanged. He told them to cleanse their hearts by ceasing to do evil and starting to do good like relieving the oppressed, judging the fatherless and pleading for the widow. (Isa 1:10-17)

On another occasion he told them that their fasting was also unacceptable. They were simply obeying instructions but there was strife in their hearts. He said that they should stop wickedness and undo the heavy burdens imposed on others, to release those who are oppressed and break every yoke of bondage. He said they should feed the hungry and bring the poor to live with them and clothe those who are naked. This he said is the true righteousness that he is looking for. (Isa 58:3-8)

The Jews of Jesus' day were going through the same rituals but their hearts were unchanged. They were trying to make themselves perfect by simply following a set of rules – the Mosaic Law. It is like trying to create an art masterpiece painting by numbers. They had no real understanding of what was required of them which was to live righteously, to love mercy and to walk humbly with God. (Mic 6:8)

Jesus quoted Isaiah when he said that the people honour him and say the right things but their heart remains untransformed and is not at all like the heart of God, which results in their religion being empty and pointless. (Mt 15:8-9)

Jesus, Paul, John the Baptist and others had to deal with this erroneous mind-set. They had to make it clear to the people that the righteousness God was looking for was not superficial obedience to a set of rules; obedience must be from the heart (Rom 6:17-18). Jesus told the scribes and Pharisees that although they appeared righteous to men, their hearts were still defiled (Mt 23:28). Although Jesus told them that no part of the law would be done away with (Mt 5:18), he emphasised the importance of believing that he had been sent by God to be their saviour and had come to show them the error of their ways, and that by believing what he said to them and obeying his instructions they would be saved.

They needed to understand that it is obedience from the heart that God seeks. When the Day of Judgment comes our bodies may have already decayed and returned to dust, but it is the spirit which returns to God (Ecc 12:7) that will be examined for similitude with God.

Jesus told Nicodemus that unless a man is born again he cannot see the kingdom of God (Jn 3:3), but Nicodemus could only understand natural birth so Jesus had to explain that he was talking about spiritual birth. He had to be born again or born from above in order to enter the kingdom of heaven. (Jn 3:5)

It is clearly of paramount importance to understand what Jesus meant by this statement yet the true meaning of it has eluded multitudes who call themselves Born Again Christians but who will never enter the kingdom of heaven unless they have their spiritual eyes opened to what it really means and repent. The church is full of people who have prayed a prayer of repentance or salvation with their mind and now consider themselves to be born again, but by their actions, or lack of them, they demonstrate that their prayer has ever been translated into heart reality.

To understand what it means to be born again we need to go right back to the creation of man.

In the beginning God created man in his own image (Gen 1:26-27). When we read that mankind was created in the image of God we must remember that God is a Spirit (Jn 4:24). Mankind was created with the same spiritual characteristics as God; such characteristics as Paul refers to as the fruit of the Spirit (Gal 5:22-23). He was a spiritual *chip off the old block*.

However, we find that when Satan came along in the form of a serpent, Adam and Eve obeyed him rather than God and so he became their lord, for Paul writes that we become the servant of whoever we obey. Obedience to the devil when tempted leads to death, but righteous acts of obedience to God lead to life (Rom 6:16).

By the time we reach the Flood of Noah's day we read that God saw how great man's wickedness had become throughout the earth, and how he was continually filled with the evil thoughts of his heart (Gen 6:5).

Man's heart had changed from being *in the image of God* as it was at creation, to being in the image of Satan, and since Amos declares that we cannot walk with God unless we are in unity with him (Amos 3:3), in other words in his image having his heart, we need to be recreated in his image. We need to be born again, or born of God from above. We need to have the Spirit of God, not the spirit of Satan. We must become children of God, not children of the devil.

John writes that whoever believes that Jesus is the Christ is born of God (1Jn 5:1), yet James concludes that if we say we have faith but there are no works of righteousness to verify it then we are no better than the demons who also believe, and our faith is not real. He says it is our works that validate our faith (Jas 2:18-20).

Belief or faith is more than an academic acceptance of truth. Jesus explains that true belief is not of the mind but of the heart or spirit.

Talking to his disciples, Jesus told them that whoever shall say to this mountain, displace yourself from here into the sea; and has no doubt in his **heart**, but believes that what he has spoken will happen; his command will be carried out. (Mk 11:23)

In his book *The Real Faith*, Dr. Charles Price writes:

In our blindness of heart and mind, we have taken faith out of the realm of the spiritual and, without realizing just what we were doing, have put it in the realm of the metaphysical. An army of emotions and desires has driven Faith from the chambers of the heart into the cold and unfruitful corridors of the mind.

With an unchanged heart obedience to God is possible only by will power, and then only for a limited time for we will always revert to our natural ways, but when we have a heart transformed or reborn in the likeness of God it will take no effort to obey because our desires will be the same as his. Then we can say with the psalmist 'I delight to do your will my God: your law is established within my heart' (Psa 40:8). Paul says that Christ must be formed **in** us. (Gal 4:19)

We have seen how obedience to God is of paramount importance. Jesus said that only those who do the will of his Father will enter the kingdom of heaven, and even though we may do many things in his name and call him Lord if we do not obey he will turn to us and say 'I never knew you.' (Mt 7:21-23)

John writes that if we obey him we know him and that if we do not obey him we do not know him (1Jn 2:3-4). Obedience is clearly the key to knowing God and being known of him.

Paul writes that when Jesus returns he will take vengeance on those who don't know God and who do not obey him, consigning them to everlasting destruction (2The 1:8-9). To Titus he writes that there are those who say they know God but by their works they show that this is untrue, being disobedient and lacking in every good work (Tit 1:16). The good works, that he says those who are saved by grace are called to walk in, are lacking (Eph 2:8-10). As Peter says, judgment will first begin at the house of God, adding that if the righteous are scarcely saved what will be the end of the disobedient? (1Pet 4:17)

It is clear that all the contributors to the New Testament scriptures acknowledge the need for works, as we have already seen through the parables of Jesus but that does not negate grace.

No! Paul writes that the grace of God which brings salvation **teaches us** that we should live soberly, righteously and in a godly way in the present world; resisting and rejecting unrighteousness and worldly passions. (Tit 2:11-12)

In some ways grace is similar to a *conditional discharge* from a court of law; it is not earned or deserved, but is given provided the recipient complies with certain conditions. Whether the recipient of that discharge (grace) ends up free or in prison depends on whether or not they comply with the conditions. Many re-offend and go back to prison because their ways have not changed. Those who have a change of heart do not re-offend and retain their liberty. This is why Paul and others give so many exhortations to change (Eph 5:6-8; Col 3:25).

The grace of God is saying that he will put our sin to one side and make heaven available to us who had no hope of entering **IF** we will cease from sin and be conformed to his image by exchanging our characteristics for his. As we have seen, this is the same grace that he made available to those under the Old Covenant. (Eze 33:11-16). God's standards do not change!

Jesus didn't die on the cross to lower the entry standard for the kingdom of heaven. He died on the cross to pay the penalty for your sin and mine, to make it possible for us to enter into the kingdom of heaven by wiping the slate clean with God. God's standards do not change. What was right in the Old Testament is still right in the New Testament, what was wrong in the Old Testament is still wrong in the New Testament. Even though the penalty for our sin has been paid in full, we are still required to live an obedient and godly life if we expect to enter the kingdom of heaven.

Paul also wrote of the need to continually restrict our fleshly desires from rising up and dominating our lives, for fear that even though we may be ministers of the gospel we may be rejected or castaway ourselves (1Cor 9:24-27). Some have associated this rejection as a loss of rewards, but the Greek word used here *adokimos* is used exclusively in the New Testament with reference to those who do not have salvation (Rom 1:28; 2Cor 13:5-7; 2Tim 3:8; Tit 1:16; Heb 6:8).

Jesus taught that the pure in heart will see God (Mt 5:8). Paul also wrote to Titus saying that to those who are pure all things are pure, but that nothing is pure to those whose lives are stained with uncleanliness and unbelief; for even their mind and conscience is stained with uncleanliness. (Tit 1:15)

The New Testament exhortations to stop doing what is wrong, and start doing what is right, are not optional. Without compliance we will be excluded from the kingdom of heaven, this is why Paul said we should work out our salvation with fear and trembling (Php 2:12), and why Jesus told us to strive to enter in (Lu 13:24).

When Jesus dictated letters to the seven churches of Asia, we have seen how he started each letter with the words *I know your works*, and ended every letter with the words *He that has an ear to hear, let him hear what the Spirit says to the churches*. He called five of them to repentance after telling them that their **works** were unacceptable, warning them of the eternal consequences of failing to repent (Rev 2&3).

Works most definitely have a part to play in our salvation. Not the superficial or ceremonial works of the laws written on stone, but the works of righteousness that proceed from and are evidence of a changed heart. Paul made this clear in his teaching to the Ephesian church on salvation by grace when he added that we are God's workmanship and are created in Christ Jesus to do good works which God had preordained for us to live by. (Eph 2:8-10)

HOW DOES GOD VIEW
TODAY'S CHURCH?

L et us first look at the origins of the church and how it should appear to God.

Back in the days of Daniel, God gave Nebuchadnezzar king of Babylon a dream. In that dream he showed him the world empires chronologically declining in nobility down through the ages, using his own empire as the starting point. They are all represented by one statue which is eventually shattered by a stone representing Jesus that, as the church, grows and fills the whole Earth. There is no place left for those earthly kingdoms, but the kingdom established by Jesus will be everlasting. (Dan 2:31-45)

Believers in the early church were described as those who were turning the world upside down (Act 17:6). Like the stone in Nebuchadnezzar's dream, they had a transforming power; today we might describe them as 'movers and shakers', but as the church has grown in numbers its impact particularly in Western European nations has been seen by many as irrelevant to today's society. This is a reversal of how it should be. Many mainstream denominational churches have reported declining numbers year on year for some considerable time. Jesus warned that in the last days before his return the love of many would grow cold because disobedience to God's laws would be widespread (Mt 24:12), but added that those who held fast to their faith right to the end would be saved (Mt 24:13).

Jesus came to transform this world by showing mankind their need and enabling them to change their lives. He shone the light into their darkness, and called his church to light up the darkness as he had done. He sent his disciples into the world to tell everyone of their need to change, and said that this was to continue until he returned (Mt 24:14).

The message is to call people out of the darkness of this world of which Babylon and its successive empires were representative, and into the light of God's kingdom; to get out of a dying kingdom and into an eternal one, as shown so graphically by *The Pilgrim's Progress*. The two kingdoms are very different, and separate. The children of God are called to be different and separate from the children of this world (2Cor 6:14-18). Yet many in the church have turned back to Egypt in their hearts (Act 7:39) they are not progressing towards their Promised Land. They have put their hand to the plough, but then turned back showing they are not fit for the kingdom of God (Lu 9:62). They have been seduced by what this world has to offer and are like the seed sown amongst the thorns (Lu 8:14) and many in *The Pilgrim's Progress*, who settled in *Vanity Fair* and never continued into the *Celestial City*. The Israelites under Joshua's leadership strived and eventually entered their Promised Land but later generations wanted to be like the kingdoms of this world that surrounded them (1Sam 8).

Why is it that men of this world see the church of today as irrelevant, when it is supposed to be salt and light (Mt 5:13-17)? Although this worldly viewpoint is not universally true, it is true in far too many places where the light is not shining and the salt has lost its effectiveness and is good for nothing.

People who are lost can often look at the church and see it not as a bright light showing the way out of darkness, but as a weak and insipid version of the world, and Christians as people who need a crutch to get through life. This is very different from Joshua's Israel and the early church that turned the world upside down. The church sometimes speaks words of separation, but then many Christians fail to obey God and don't follow his ways, they emulate the sinful ways of people in the world or live by worldly principles and standards.

Paul lists many works of the flesh which will preclude entry to the kingdom of God (Gal 5:19-21), but sadly these are all to be found to one degree or another inside the church. Who do we think we are kidding if we live in such a way? We don't fool God, and the people of this world see right through us. The only ones we are deceiving are ourselves.

Not only do many continue in these works of the flesh, but they often try to hide them and think that nobody will notice. Those who are in bed with the world will receive the same judgment as the world, whether they call themselves Christians or not (Eph 5:6-8).

We are called the temple of God, his dwelling place, but he does not live in a hovel. We must cleanse our temple as the Levites did in Hezekiah's day (2Chr 29:1-19). We must separate ourselves from the unrighteous worldly associations in our lives as depicted by the mixed marriages of Ezra's day and Nehemiah's day (Ezra 10; Neh 13:1-3). We must return to God's standards of holiness as they did in Josiah's day (2Kin 22-23). We must cease to be joined to Tobiah who depicts the worldly influence of the devil (Neh 6:17-19) and remove him from our temple and cleanse it (Neh 13:4-9) and have nothing to do with the unfruitful works of the evil one (Eph 5:11).

We must be like Jesus and cleanse our temple from worldly influence, separating ourselves from worldly thoughts and ways (Mt 21:12-13; Jn 2:13-16).

As Paul wrote, we must put off our old ways, have our minds changed, and put on God's ways as we would spiritually change from dirty old rags to fine clean clothes (Eph 4:22-24).

Many do not exhibit the characteristics of God such as selfless love or compassion, they are still selfish. They say God has given us all things richly to enjoy (1Tim 6:17) so they live in pleasures whilst their brothers and sisters elsewhere in the world are struggling for their very existence. They might even throw a million dollar crumb in their direction; but whilst Jesus in our brothers and sisters still has need, can we live in plenty like the *Rich Man* in Jesus' parable (Lu 16:19-31) and still believe that we are really the children of God (1Jn 3:17; Jas 2:15-16)? We would do well to consider the actions of the early church in this respect who sold what they had so that those that had need could be supported (Act 2:44-45, 4:34-37).

Does God not grieve when he sees so many in the church entertaining themselves with the trivial pursuits of this world when he has given us work to do, and when millions of his creation are going to hell because the church wants to enjoy itself more than it is committed to convert and pray for the souls of the lost?

Does the church spend more time being happy and rejoicing in their own salvation even praising God inside four walls than it does in doing the will of God by shining their light outside in the darkness of this world so that more souls can find their way into the kingdom?

God is not pleased with our selfish and hard-hearted indifference to the needs of others (Isa 1:11-17). There is a time to be happy and a time to be sad (Ecc 3:1-4). Can we really rejoice when God is grieving for lost souls that **we** are letting perish (Joel 1)?

Have many in today's church lost the plot?

Paul talks of aiding our brothers and sisters in their ministries in any way that we can *as is appropriate action for those who are saints or holy ones* (Rom 16:2), yet there are some who call themselves brothers or sisters that impede their fellow workers or charge them for services where they could easily assist for the sake of the work and the kingdom. This kind of attitude belongs to the empire builders of **this** world, not to those of the kingdom of God – freely you have received, freely give (Mt 10:8; 1Pet 5:2).

SUMMARY OF JESUS' TEACHINGS

We can read these parables of Jesus and even understand them, yet not associate with them for ourselves. If the cap fits – wear it!

The message of Jesus' sayings is crystal clear, and yet many in the church have failed to take heed, preferring rather to trust presumptuously in promises for which they have not met the qualifying conditions. It is oh so easy to accept the work of Christ and rejoice in what he has done without even realizing that we all have a part to play in our own salvation; it is not all **his work**. His work is finished, now it is our work. We clearly have a part to play in our own salvation.

So what is our part? Jesus said that the work we must do is to **believe** on him whom God has sent (Jn 6:29); this is not an intellectual acceptance of fact, it is not an academic exercise, but rather that we should take heed to what he has said and do it (Mt 7:24).

If you were warned that an approaching tsunami would flood your low lying coastal village within 24 hours and that many people would be drowned, then if you truly believed you would take appropriate action.

We have seen how God spoke through Ezekiel and said that even though the death sentence may have been pronounced, anyone who takes corrective action will not die (Eze 33:14-16).

However, before you believe, you need to assess the authority of whoever is giving the warning. This book has given you a warning and is based on more than 750 scriptures and founded on the teachings of Jesus; you must assess its authority.

Let us remind ourselves of the authority of Jesus' words, for there is no higher authority.

As we have already seen, God spoke to Moses telling him that he would send a prophet like him, a deliverer. This prophet would speak the words of God and the people must listen to what he says or answer to God for failing to do so (Deu 18:15-19). Moslems are taught that this refers to Mohammad, but he doesn't accurately fit the description.

When Jesus came in fulfilment of this word, he said that he only spoke the words the Father gave him (Jn 12:49-50), and only did those things he saw his Father do (Jn 5:19).

God spoke from heaven in confirmation saying this is my beloved Son in whom I am well pleased, **HEAR YE HIM** (Mt 17:5). Listen to what he tells you because he is my messenger to you and he will tell you how you can be saved (Jn 6:63, 68).

We read that Jesus has been given all authority, (Mt 28:18) and that he will be our judge. (Act 10:42) So then, because Jesus our judge speaks the words of the highest authority, a wise man will listen carefully and take appropriate action, for his eternal salvation depends on it.

Let us try to summarize all that Jesus has said to us.

First and foremost, remember that God is calling the shots, and Jesus said that only those who do the will of God will enter the kingdom of heaven.

We must watch for the signs of his coming and be ready for him when he comes, otherwise we will be excluded from the kingdom of heaven.

If we turn up to the wedding without putting on our wedding garment, which is a robe of righteousness, then we will be excluded from the kingdom of heaven. Our righteousness is the wedding garment of the saints or holy ones; it is not worn externally, but it is of the heart or spirit of man. It can be seen by our lifestyle and actions, - works of righteousness proceeding from a transformed heart. This is what it truly means to be born again, and as Jesus told Nicodemus, if we are not born again we will never even see the kingdom of heaven, let alone enter it.

We must be born again because we must become compatible with God if we want to walk with him (Amos 3:3). We must have clean hands and a pure heart if we want to ascend into heaven (Psa 24:3). We must live righteously if we want to remain in heaven (Psa 15:1).

We must be doing the work of the kingdom for which we have been called; even in the face of persecution and adversity we must still shine our light. We must not fear man who can kill our body, but fear God who can destroy body and soul in hell fire. If we deny Jesus before man, then he will deny knowing us before his Father. It is the Father's will that we be working in and for his kingdom; those who are not doing Father's will do not enter the kingdom of heaven (Mt 7:21).

Our lives must show that we have love and compassion otherwise it will show that we have not been transformed, we will still be like the *Rich Man* and the *Goats* and will be excluded from the kingdom of heaven, for it demonstrates a selfish rather than a selfless heart.

We must be merciful and forgiving otherwise our heavenly Father will not forgive us, and we will not enter the kingdom of heaven.

In short we must have the character traits of God. Jesus was the express image of the Father, and we must become the image of God's Son. These character traits are what Paul refers to as the fruit of the Spirit, and unless we bear fruit of this kind we will be cast into the lake of fire and burned (Jn 15:1-8).

The warnings that Jesus has given are to those whose lives do not demonstrate the good works that he has told us about. These works of righteousness show us and the world that our heart has been transformed and is now once again in tune with God.

In the beginning we were created with these character traits of God, but when Adam and Eve disobeyed God and obeyed the devil in the guise of a serpent, those traits began to change and mankind became the servants of the devil (Rom 6:16).

By the time of the great Flood of Noah's day men's hearts had changed so much that God had to destroy his creation and start again. Even then mankind continued to turn away from God and follow the devil, but when Jesus came he taught us that we need to revert back to how we were in the day of our creation.

We need to be recreated or reborn having the Spirit of God in us, not the spirit of this world which is of the devil; it is self-seeking. We read that friendship of the world is enmity with God (Jas 4:4), and that if we love the world, the love of the Father is not in us (1Jn 2:15). Paul writes that we must not be conformed to this world which is the spirit of Babylon, but be transformed by having our minds renewed to think and then act as God does (Rom 12:2).

Now God is love and everyone who has this same characteristic is born of God (1Jn 4:7-8). God is light and in him there is no darkness, but if we do not love our brother then we are still in darkness, and therefore cannot be in God, for darkness is not compatible with light, they cannot co-exist. So without love we will not enter the kingdom of heaven.

We must become like God. Not in the same way that Satan wanted to become like God, in power and authority for that was just self-exaltation. We must want to emulate him and have his ways and his thoughts (Isa 55:7-8). We do this by a process of exchange, exchanging our ways for his; replacing selfishness with selflessness.

Jesus told two short parables; *The Treasure* and *The Pearl* (Mt 13:44-46). These both tell us of this need to exchange what we consider to be valuable by this world's standards, and in their place to receive the true riches of the kingdom of heaven. We cannot have both (Mt 6:24). Jesus taught this same principle when he said we should not store up treasure on earth like *The Rich Fool*, but store up true treasure in heaven (Mt 6:19-21). Natural riches are in stark contrast with spiritual riches. (Rev 2:9, 3:17)

Jesus said that we should be perfect, just as our Father which is in heaven is perfect. (Mt 5:48)

We are commanded to be holy; because God is holy (1 Pet 1:16). Without holiness, no man shall see the Lord (Heb 12:14).We would do well to consider the Holiness churches of yesteryear, and notice how far some of today's churches have moved away from God's standards of holiness.

There is a battle taking place for your soul. The devil is tempting you through the weakness of your flesh to indulge in the pleasures of this world, but this leads you into sin which ends in death (Jas 1:14-15) and separation from God. God is appealing to your spirit so that you might live righteously and live with him throughout eternity.

Paul wrote that those who yield to the desires of the flesh are concerned with matters of the flesh; but they that are led by the Spirit the matters of the Spirit and the kingdom of God. For the worldly mind leads to death; but the spiritually minded have life and peace. The worldly mind is in opposition to God, for it is not subject to the law of God, neither can it be; so those who are in the flesh cannot please God (Rom 8:5-8).

If we are serious about entering the kingdom of God we will say NO to worldly distractions and temptations.

If you allow your fleshly desires to dominate your life you will die; but if through the Spirit you put to death the deeds of the flesh, you will live. For those who allow the Spirit of God to lead them are the sons of God. (Rom 8:13-14)

It is only the sons of God who will enter the kingdom of God.

Are you truly ready for the Lord's return? There are many who believe that it is imminent. Review your life and see yourself through the eyes of God using these sayings of Jesus and make sure you are ready.

Jesus said we should strive to enter in. The author of Hebrews urges us not to make the same mistake that the Israelites of Moses' day did when he calls us to make haste to enter in (Heb 4:11).

Don't allow the devil to tempt you to backslide from God's standard like those who entered the *Vanity Fair* of *John Bunyan's 'The Pilgrim's Progress'*, for it is only those who endure to the end who shall be saved (Mt 24:13). Jesus said that if we put our hand to the plough and turn back we are not fit for the kingdom of God (Lu 9:62) and warned us to remember Lot's wife (Lu 17:32) who, looking back, perished. I would urge you to read the whole of the book of Hebrews from the point of view of enduring.

Jesus gave us the parable of **The Sower** (Mt 13:3-9, 18-23). This story tells us that there were four different types of ground representing the hearts of men. They **all** received the seed which is the word of God, but **only one** bore fruit. The seed by the wayside did not take root at all, the seed on stony ground started joyfully but as it did not have a strong root system when temptation, trouble or persecution came the seed withered and died. When the cares of this world, the deceitfulness of riches or the pleasures of this world entered in to the heart, the seed sown amongst the thorns withered and died. It was only the seed that was sown into good ground that produced fruit, without which the fire awaits.

Jesus implied that we need to understand this parable properly to understand all the parables (Mk 4:13). This parable identifies the spiritual birth process. It is similar to the natural birth process, except that which is born of the flesh is flesh, and that which is born of the Spirit is spirit (Jn 3:6). When a woman receives the seed of a man she does not immediately give birth, nor is birth a certainty. There may be no egg present for the seed to fertilize (seed by the wayside). Conception may take place but the egg may not be firmly attached to the wall of the womb (seed on stony ground). The woman may miscarry or abort (seed among the thorns); or she may continue to the end and birth the child.

Many people say they are born again when in fact they have only received the seed, Jesus, the word of God. They have been conceived and are in the birth process, but this parable identifies the causes that may prevent them from coming to the birth. John writes that those who receive Jesus, the seed, have the ability **to become** the sons of God, it's not automatic (Jn 1:12-13). Many never climb above the bottom rung of that ladder which would take them into the kingdom of heaven.

We refer to the Bible as the canon of scripture. This Greek word *kanon* is a rule, which we can measure ourselves against and by it know whether we have eternal life. James says it is like looking in a mirror; the foolish man looks into the mirror, sees what is yet to be put right and promptly forgets (Jas 1:23-24), but a wise man is not so deceived, for he is a doer of the word (Jas 1:22).

Now you have read the scriptures in this book, use them as a mirror to look into your own spirit and see where you still lack, or whether you can truly say you have the heart of God. May God bless you and lead you into a true and enduring relationship with him through Jesus Christ *The Way*.

Before you put this book down, finish by reading this modern day parable and then consider how you think God will respond to those that call themselves his sons but live a life of self-gratification, for this story is similar in parts to the vision given to William Booth.

The crude lifesaving station *by Theodore Wedel*

On a dangerous seacoast where shipwrecks often occur, there was once a crude little lifesaving station. The building was no more than a hut, and there was only one boat; but the few devoted members kept a constant watch over the sea. With no thought for themselves, they went out day and night, tirelessly searching for the lost. Some of those who had been saved, and various others in the surrounding area, wanted to be associated with the station and give their time, money, and effort to support the work. New boats were bought and new crews trained. The little lifesaving station grew.

Some of these new members of the lifesaving station were unhappy that the building was so crude and poorly equipped. They felt that a more comfortable place should be provided as the first refuge of those who were saved from the sea. They replaced the emergency cots with beds and put better furniture in the enlarged building. Now the lifesaving station became a popular gathering place for its members, and they decorated it beautifully and furnished it exqui-sitely because they used it as a sort of club. Fewer members were now interested in going to sea on lifesaving missions, so they hired lifeboat crews to do this work. The lifesaving motif still prevailed in this club's decoration, and there was a memorial lifeboat in the room where the club initiations were held.

About this time a large ship was wrecked off the coast, and the hired crews brought in boatloads of cold, wet, half-drowned people. They were dirty and sick, and some of them were foreigners. The beautiful new club was in chaos. Immediately, the property committee hired someone to rig up a shower house outside the club, where victims of ship-wrecks could be cleaned up before coming inside.

At the next meeting, there was a split in the club mem-bership. Most of the members wanted to stop the club's life-saving activities because they felt they were unpleasant and a hindrance to the normal social life of the club. A small number of members insisted upon lifesaving as their primary purpose and pointed out that they were still called a life-saving station. The small group's members were voted down and told that if they wanted to save lives, they could begin their own lifesaving station down the coast.

They did.

As the years went by, however, the new station expe-rienced the same changes that had occurred in the old sta-tion. It evolved into a club, and yet another lifesaving station was founded. History continued to repeat itself, and if you visit that seacoast today, you will find a number of exclusive clubs along that shore.

Shipwrecks are frequent in those waters, but most of the passengers drown.

Lightning Source UK Ltd.
Milton Keynes UK
UKOW050605170911

178831UK00002B/2/P